Contents

Economic Management of Marine Living Resources

A Practical Introduction

David Whitmarsh

publishing for a sustainable future

London • Washington, DC

First published in 2011 by Earthscan

Copyright © Professor David Whitmarsh 2011

The moral right of the author has been asserted.

All rights reserved. No part of this publication may be reproduced, stored in a retrieval system, or transmitted, in any form or by any means, electronic, mechanical, photocopying, recording or otherwise, except as expressly permitted by law, without the prior, written permission of the publisher.

Earthscan Ltd, Dunstan House, 14a St Cross Street, London EC1N 8XA, UK
Earthscan LLC, 1616 P Street, NW, Washington, DC 20036, USA

Earthscan publishes in association with the International Institute for Environment and Development

For more information on Earthscan publications, see www.earthscan.co.uk or write to earthinfo@earthscan.co.uk

ISBN: 978-1-84971-258-3 hardback
ISBN: 978-1-84971-259-0 paperback

Typeset by 4word Ltd
Cover design by Susanne Harris

A catalogue record for this book is available from the British Library

Library of Congress Cataloging-in-Publication Data

Whitmarsh, David.
  Economic management of marine living resources : a practical introduction / David Whitmarsh.
    p. cm.
  Includes bibliographical references and index.
  ISBN 978-1-84971-258-3 (hardback)
  1. Marine resources—Economic aspects. 2. Marine resources—Management. 3. Marine resources conservation. I. Title.
  GC1018.5.W55 2010
  333.95'6—dc22   2010036269

At Earthscan we strive to minimize our environmental impacts and carbon footprint through reducing waste, recycling and offsetting our CO_2 emissions, including those created through publication of this book. For more details of our environmental policy, see www.earthscan.co.uk.

Printed and bound in the UK by TJ International Ltd, Padstow, Cornwall.

The paper used is FSC certified and the inks are vegetable based.

FSC
www.fsc.org
MIX
Paper from
responsible sources
FSC® C013056

List of Figures and Tables

Figures

Tables

List of Acronyms and Abbreviations

AHP	analytic hierarchy process
CBA	cost-benefit analysis
CEA	cost-effectiveness analysis
CFZ	coastal fishery zone
CI	Consistency Index
CPUE	catch per unit of effort
CR	Consistency Ratio
CV	contingent valuation
CVM	contingent valuation method
DCF	discounted cash flow
DWFN	distant water fishing nation
EAF	ecosystem approaches to fisheries management
E_{mey}	effort level at which economic yield is maximized
E_{msy}	effort at which maximum sustainable yield is achieved
E_{oa}	open-access effort level
EU	European Union
FAO	UN Food and Agriculture Organization
FCR	food conversion ratio
FIGIS	Fisheries Information Global System
GS	Gordon-Schaefer
HABs	harmful algal blooms
IQ	individual quota
IRR	internal rate of return
ITOPF	International Tanker Owners Pollution Federation
ITQ	individual transferable quota
LIFDCs	low income food deficit countries
MCA	multi-criteria analysis
MCS	Marine Conservation Society
MEY	maximum economic yield
MEZ	marine exclusion zone
MPA	marine protected area

MSC	Marine Stewardship Council
MSY	maximum sustainable yield
NPV	net present value
NTZ	no-take zone
OA	open-access
p.a.	per annum
TAC	total allowable catch
TURF	territorial user right in fishing
WTP	willingness to pay

Preface

Rationale and main themes

This textbook has two main objectives. Firstly, it outlines the problems associated with the management and conservation of marine living resources, with particular attention given to the twin concepts of economic value and socio-economic sustainability. It aims to demonstrate the contribution that economics can make to understanding these problems, as well as in helping to frame policies to mitigate them. Secondly, it looks in detail at the key methods that may be used to collect and analyse socio-economic data, oriented towards the information needs of decision makers and stakeholders involved in fisheries management. Together, these two objectives address the question: how does society make the best use of its marine living resources?

The notion of 'best use' is central to economics, which is concerned with the problem of how to satisfy human wants in the face of scarcity. One of the implications of scarcity is the need to make choices between alternative uses of limited resources (human, man-made and natural) in the production of goods and services. Indeed, the subject is sometimes referred to as the 'science of choice', and most economics textbooks invariably include sections explaining how people make choices under a given set of conditions. This theme recurs throughout the present book, and features in several chapters. It will become clear, for example, that marine resource managers face choices both in the objectives they are trying to pursue (which might include environmental protection as well as livelihood support) and the instruments they use to achieve them (such as area closures or restrictive vessel licensing). But we are interested too in the choices made by all those involved in the process of production and consumption, since this gives us a guide to some of the problems that resource managers must tackle. Choices are influenced by incentives, and much of the concern here is in seeing how the behaviour of producers and households can be modified to ensure that the choices they make are optimal from the standpoint of the community at large. One of the problems we shall look at is that fishermen may find it worthwhile carrying on their operations even when a fishery is over-exploited, suggesting that there is something wrong with the incentive structure. Consumers may similarly have no reason to change their behaviour if there are no market signals, either through price or from product labelling, to indicate that the particular variety of fish they are about to purchase is from an unsustainable source. Economics can help to shape policies that alter this state of affairs so as to ensure that the choices that people make are consistent with the best interests of society as a whole.

Coverage and intended readership

The book is structured around seven key topics, commencing with an overview of the economic significance of marine living resources and then focusing on specific problems that are typically encountered by resource managers. It has a strong practical emphasis, and draws upon case studies from both developed and developing countries. The primary audience will comprise undergraduate and postgraduate students with an interest in the fisheries and aquaculture sector and its role in the economy. However, attention is also given to non-market goods, including the value of critical marine habitats such as mangroves, sea grasses and corals. The book is aimed mainly at those with little background in economics, studying environmental science, marine conservation, geography and coastal zone management. Hopefully it will also be of value to practitioners, particularly policy-makers with responsibility for resolving conflicts and managing marine fisheries in the wider context of multiple resource use.

The book was written because it was felt that there is no text that satisfactorily meets the needs of students at an introductory level on the economics of marine living resources. While there are some excellent books and monographs which go into considerable analytical detail on important areas such as the overfishing problem and the valuation of marine environmental assets, arguably these are too advanced for those who have no prior knowledge of economics. At the other end of the spectrum, nowadays there are some very good introductory texts covering the wider subject area of environmental and resource economics, but these typically give relatively little coverage to the marine environment or to fisheries. Having in recent years worked closely with marine scientists on various research projects, and also run several short-course training programmes on socio-economic aspects of fisheries management, I now have a rather clearer picture of what non-economists both wish to know and need to know about the subject. This experience has shaped the topic coverage of the book. The only assumption I have made is that readers have at least a basic familiarity with statistical methods.

Acknowledgements

I owe an important intellectual debt to past and present members of the Department of Economics, University of Portsmouth, and particularly to its specialist research group CEMARE (the Centre for the Economics and Management of Aquatic Resources). The collaboration I have had with the group over a period of some 37 years has inevitably meant that I have enjoyed the friendship and encouragement of many people, and I trust I will be forgiven if I do not mention all of them here. However, those to whom I am especially grateful are my former colleagues Steve Cunningham, Mike Dunn, Arthur Neiland, Sean Pascoe, Alan Radford and Jimmy Young. I also wish to acknowledge the assistance of the Earthscan production team, particularly Tim Hardwick, as well as the comments of several anonymous reviewers. Penultimately, I would like to thank my family for their love and support, and for tolerating my preoccupation with working on this book when I should perhaps have been gainfully employed on the domestic front. Finally, I would like to give special thanks to my daughter, Lorraine, for helping with the final amendments to this text. I am sure that without this, the book would have been unlikely to see the light of day.

1
Marine Living Resources and Their Economic Significance

1.1 Introduction

The oceans cover some three-quarters of the globe and support a diversity of living resources that sustain the livelihoods of millions of people across all continents. In this chapter we will look at how these resources are used in production and consumption, and more generally what makes them important in social and economic terms. The main focus, however, is on the challenges faced by the marine fisheries sector, and their implications for particular groups of people and nation states. Some of these challenges, notably the over-exploitation of fish stocks, can be regarded as *endogenous*, since they arise from within the fisheries sector itself – although, as we will make clear, this may have been worsened by external factors in the form of government-supported initiatives such as subsidies and encouragement to adopt new technology. These challenges may be compounded by events which originate outside the fisheries sector (i.e. they are *exogenous*), of which climate change is surely the most recent and prominent. Major environmental disturbances, such as pollution incidents and 'red tides', also come into this category and will be discussed in a later chapter.

We have suggested that one of the aims in this chapter is to assess the socio-economic importance of marine living resources, and because this is a theme that runs throughout the book, it is appropriate to briefly consider what this means. To start with, we need to recognize that 'importance' is a relative concept, and as such it will involve making comparisons. At its simplest this could be done by choosing some indicator such as fish landings and comparing current with past levels in order to gauge trends, or else by comparing different countries or continents in a given year. In many respects, however, the more interesting (but more difficult) issues involve comparisons between where we are now and where we might otherwise be. For example, questions such as

'How far are current landings below their maximum?', 'How much economic waste is there in the fisheries?', and 'What is the damage caused to fisheries by an oil spill?', invite a comparison between an actual situation and some alternative state which may not be easy to measure empirically. In this situation, economic importance becomes equated with the magnitude of the total loss to society arising from inefficiency or from a particular event impacting adversely on the system. However, we need to be clear also from whose perspective the issue is being assessed. Overfishing may in the extreme lead to the collapse or total closure of a fishery, and this will impact differentially on the multiple interest or stakeholder groups involved. The same is true of extreme events such as oil spills, illustrated by the unfolding drama of the Deepwater Horizon oil spill in the Gulf of Mexico in 2010, in which the pollution incident itself and the immediate response impacted most harshly on local fishermen, but were also felt by seafood retailers and consumers throughout the US. The question in this case concerns not just the magnitude of damages but also their incidence – an issue of *equity*. In short, we cannot meaningfully answer the question of economic importance without some qualification: importance *for whom*?

These are ideas that will make their appearance here, but which recur in later chapters and indeed represent much of the sub-text of the whole book. We start by looking at the economic functions of the marine environment, followed by a description of the global fisheries sector, its development over the past half-century and its main economic characteristics. This provides the backdrop to the theme of the following chapter, the problem of overfishing and how it may be tackled. The role of aquaculture in meeting the potential shortfall in world fish supplies is discussed, though as we point out, the rapid growth of this sector has come at an environmental cost. Finally, we consider the implications of climate change for the fisheries sector, and the extent to which countries differ in their vulnerability to climate-induced changes in fisheries.

1.2 Economic functions of the marine environment

The marine environment fulfils two basic functions in regard to society. First, it provides natural resources that are used to produce a range of valuable goods and services. These include physical commodities such as fishery products, amenity benefits associated with recreation, and also a range of important ecosystem services covering water purification, biodiversity protection and natural coastal defence (Brown et al, 2002). Secondly, the marine environment acts as a depository or sink for the waste products of human activity, such as water and materials that may have undergone some degree of treatment (as in the case of sewage) or recycling prior to discharge and deposition.

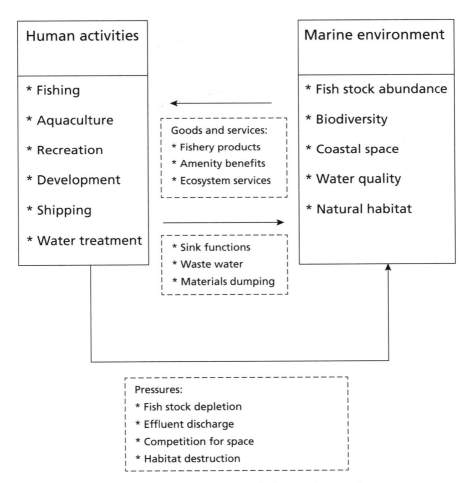

Figure 1.1 *Human activities and the marine environment*

The demand for marine products, and likewise the rate at which wastes are deposited in the sea, are directly related to economic activity (Figure 1.1). Rising per capita income and population will translate into increasing food consumption, which for many countries is likely to include seafood products. Other activities such as shipping and marine leisure (yachting, recreational fishing) are also driven to a large extent by economic conditions and the general affluence of society. The crucial point, however, is that both these functions – natural resource provision and waste removal – impose pressures and impacts on the marine environment which may ultimately jeopardize its sustainability. These impacts include: potentially harmful discharges of organic and chemical effluents; competition for space in congested coastal areas; and destruction of critical habitat such as mangrove and submerged aquatic vegetation. (The reader should note that depletion of fish stocks *per se* can be, but is not necessarily, unsustainable.) To understand these issues, therefore, we need to have some appreciation of how the economy interacts with the marine environment. In the present chapter we focus on fisheries and their depletion, and address some of the other themes later.

1.3 Capture fisheries and aquaculture

1.3.1 Overview

Global production data for the year 2007, from the two main sources of supply, capture fisheries and aquaculture, are given in Table 1.1. These data refer to reported fisheries statistics, and may not fully reveal the true economic and social effects of fishing worldwide, due to high levels of illegal catches (Agnew and Barnes, 2003). Capture fisheries account for some 60 per cent of the total, within which marine fish species were the largest category. Aquaculture, which is the farming of fish and aquatic organisms, is more dependent on freshwater than marine fish. The importance of aquatic plants (principally macroalgae such as Laminaria) and molluscs within the aquaculture is also noteworthy. Table 1.1 also shows clearly the role of the fisheries sector in developing countries, which accounted for over 70 per cent of production by capture fisheries and some 93 per cent of supplies from aquaculture. China has a particularly dominant role in aquaculture production. Looking more closely at marine fish, we can again see that there are quite marked differences between developed and developing countries in terms of particular species groups (Table 1.2). Demersal varieties such as cod accounted for a higher proportion of capture fisheries production for developed countries than for developing countries, while the latter were more dependent on pelagics.

International trade data provide further information on the economic significance of aquatic resources (Table 1.3). Fisheries products

Table 1.1 Global production from capture fisheries and aquaculture, 2007

Product group	Capture (tonnes)		Aquaculture (tonnes)	
	Developed countries	Developing countries	Developed countries	Developing countries
Aquatic plants	383,949	720,999	516,861	14,341,930
Crustaceans	1,164,092	4,675,990	59,997	4,828,896
Diadromous fish	1,187,199	597,486	1,490,044	1,818,173
Freshwater fish	319,681	8,397,842	537,518	26,230,613
Marine fish	19,803,894	45,840,002	433,735	1,417,730
Miscellaneous	74,732	385,498	10,400	432,533
Molluscs	2,127,827	5,436,407	1,465,964	11,605,636
Total	25,061,374	66,054,224	4,514,519	60,675,511

Note: Excludes whales and marine mammals
Source: FAO (2010a)

Table 1.2 *Global production of marine fishes, 2007*

Species group	Capture (tonnes)		Aquaculture (tonnes)	
	Developed countries	Developing countries	Developed countries	Developing countries
Cods, hakes, haddocks	7,331,690	983,703	12,212	0
Flounders, halibuts, soles	694,824	222,859	13,411	113,102
Herrings, sardines, anchovies	5,602,368	14,108,091	0	0
Marine fish not identified	481,200	8,996,441	13,699	313,383
Miscellaneous coastal fish	793,174	5,714,170	226,721	906,166
Miscellaneous demersal fish	743,920	2,169,774	0	35,979
Miscellaneous pelagic fish	2,867,942	7,851,289	162,707	43,682
Sharks, rays, chimaeras	196,744	583,940	0	0
Tunas, bonitos, billfishes	1,092,032	5,209,735	4985	5418
Total	19,803,894	45,840,002	433,735	1,417,730

Source: FAO (2010a)

Table 1.3 *International trade in fishery products, 2006*

Commodity	Developed countries		Developing countries	
	Exports ($m)	Imports ($m)	Exports ($m)	Imports ($m)
Aquatic plants	142	514	506	173
Crustaceans	6875	18,146	12,894	2169
Diadromous fish	8302	9930	3342	1097
Freshwater fish	907	2345	1671	182
Marine fish	23,875	34,703	19,192	12,479
Miscellaneous	252	590	195	322
Molluscs	3441	6421	4775	1762
Total	43,794	72,649	42,574	18,184

Note: Excludes whales and marine mammals
Source: FAO (2010a)

are an important source of foreign exchange for many countries, especially for those in developing parts of the world with a strong export orientation. As Table 1.3 shows, the value of fisheries exports from developing countries was more than double the value of their fisheries imports. The trade flow in fisheries products generally is from less developed to more developed countries, with almost three-quarters of the total import value concentrated on Japan, the US and the EU (FAO, 2009). Marine fish and crustaceans are the major product categories in international trade, the latter dominated by shrimp, which alone accounted for one-quarter of the total export earnings of all developing countries in 2006. This reliance on a single species as a generator of foreign exchange earnings has proved problematic for certain countries (e.g. Thailand), due to the volatility of shrimp prices on the international market.

1.3.2 Trends in production and consumption

Global supplies from the catching sector increased rapidly throughout the 1950s and 1960s, growing at some 6 per cent per annum (Figure 1.2). The rapid expansion of world capture fisheries in these two decades can be attributed to both supply and demand influences (Thorpe et al, 2007). On the supply side there have been important technological developments, notably: (i) synthetic fibres in net construction, accompanied by mechanization of gear hauling; (ii) increasingly sophisticated methods of fish location (e.g. sonar); and (iii) freezing at sea together with changes in vessel design to increase the range of vessel operations. In many countries, the adoption of new technology has been facilitated by financial support in the form of publicly funded grants and loans for vessel construction and modernization. On the demand side, the main drivers have

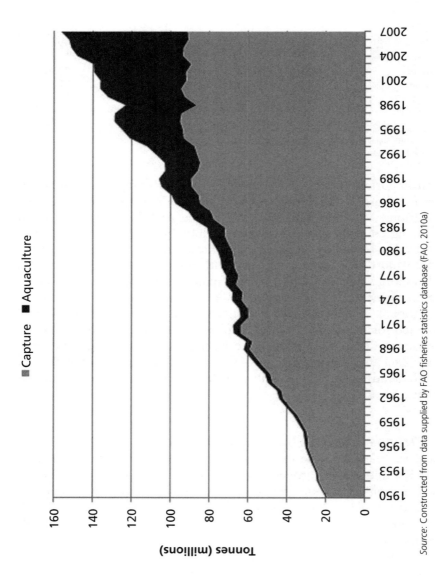

Source: Constructed from data supplied by FAO fisheries statistics database (FAO, 2010a)

Figure 1.2 *Global production: capture fisheries and aquaculture*

been growth of the world economy (implying higher per capita incomes and the ability to purchase foodstuffs) and rising total population. The levelling-off which occurred after 1970 is a reflection of the fact that most fishing areas have reached their maximum potential, while in some fisheries, landings have fallen as a result of over-exploitation. In recent years there are clear signs that global production from capture fisheries has remained static, but we know from other evidence that falls have been especially marked for particular species groups of marine fish. In complete contrast, production from aquaculture has grown rapidly throughout the period, and now accounts for well over 40 per cent of total world supplies.

There are a number of economic explanations for the reversal of fortunes in capture fisheries, but here we focus on just two. On the one hand, the degree of technological change has been such that, while it contributed to the initial expansion of world fisheries, it has also led to the growth of excess harvesting capacity and unsustainable fishing pressure (Cunningham et al, 1985). The 'double-edged sword' nature of technical innovation in fisheries is illustrated quite dramatically in the case of herring in the north-east Atlantic, where the rapid adoption of new fishing methods (notably purse seining and pelagic trawling) during the 1960s and 1970s undoubtedly led to the over-exploitation that resulted in the near-collapse and closure of the main fishing areas in the North Sea and west of Scotland in the late 1970s (Whitmarsh et al, 1995). Secondly, it is widely agreed that particular forms of government financial support for fishing – specifically, subsidies that reduce the cost of inputs such as fuel, or which offer aid to vessel construction and modernization – have exacerbated the overfishing problem by keeping global harvesting capacity and fishing effort artificially high. In recent years a number of estimates of the scale of subsidies to fishing have been made, one early study by Milazzo (1998) putting it at $14–20 billion per annum, while a more recent analysis calculates the total amount of 'overfishing' subsidies in the range of $20–26 billion p.a. (Sumaila et al, 2007).

Despite the apparent levelling-off and decline in some sectors, notably marine capture fisheries, per capita availability of fish for consumption has nearly doubled from just below 10kg p.a. in the early 1960s to over 16kg p.a. in 2005 (FAO, 2009). However, there continue to be very wide disparities in food availability between countries, and it is a matter of concern that per capita fish supply, in low-income food deficit countries excluding China (LIFDCs), in 2005 was only slightly over 8kg p.a. The pattern of consumption in 175 countries in 2003–5 is presented in Figure 1.3, which shows a very skewed distribution. A small minority of countries (5 per cent) had an exceptionally high level of fish consumption (greater than 150 grams per person per day, equivalent to

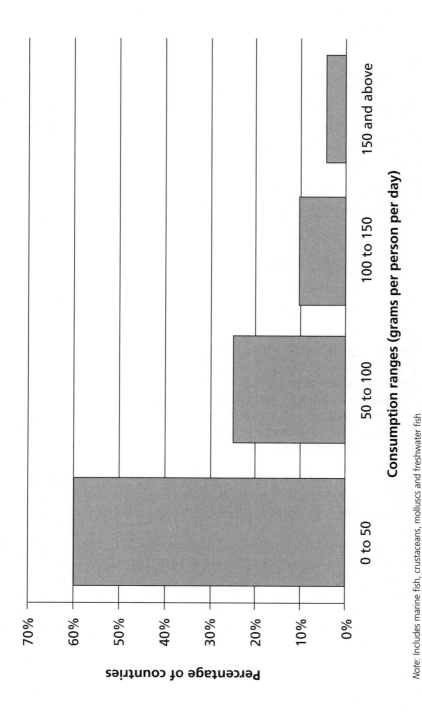

Note: Includes marine fish, crustaceans, molluscs and freshwater fish
Source: Constructed from data supplied given in FAO food security database (FAO, 2010b)

Figure 1.3 *Fish consumption across different countries, 2003–5*

54.8kg per annum), and included Malaysia, the Seychelles, Portugal, Japan, Samoa, Kiribati, Iceland and the Maldives. It is revealing to look at the changes that have taken place since the early 1990s, and to examine the number of countries that have reported increases or decreases in fish consumption. Average per capita fish supply across all countries increased over the period 1990–92 to 2003–5 by some 11 per cent. However, the experiences of individual countries underlying this summary statistic have differed. The FAO data show that of the reporting countries, the split was: increased fish consumption in 62 per cent; no change in 8 per cent; and decreased consumption in 30 per cent. While overall there appear to have been improvements in the availability of fish for human consumption, the gains have not been uniform, and for some countries the situation has deteriorated.

1.3.3 Variability in fisheries

The broad trends in global capture fisheries conceal substantial year-to-year variations in catches that may occur in individual fisheries. These are caused by: (i) fluctuations in the marine environment, which may alter the size of the fish population; and (ii) changes in fishing intensity in response to commercial opportunities. There is an interaction between these two sets of influences, which for some fisheries can give rise to a complex dynamic pattern of development that makes it difficult to predict catches from one year to the next (Charles, 2001). It also greatly complicates the task of managing certain fisheries, particularly those characterized by contrasting periods of high stock abundance alternating with near disappearance of the resource (Caddy and Gulland, 1983).

One of the best known examples of this kind of extreme variability is the Peruvian anchoveta fishery, whose catches are a major raw material input used in the fishmeal industry. Landings of anchoveta over the past half-century have fluctuated dramatically, caused in large part by the oceanic disturbance known as 'El Niño'. An especially severe El Niño event took place in the early 1970s, as a result of which landings fell precipitately to just 15 per cent of their 1971 level over a two-year period (Figure 1.4). The collapse was almost certainly caused in part, however, by a build-up in catching capacity in the preceding years, which made the fish stock more vulnerable to environmental shocks. Such volatility has important economic consequences, reflected in the price of fishmeal on the international commodity market. Anchoveta is one of a number of 'industrial' pelagic species (others include menhaden, sardine and sprat) used in fishmeal, a major feedstuff in pig and poultry farming and also salmon aquaculture. For purposes of price analysis, it is appropriate to consider changes in total supplies of these fish, and in Figure 1.5 we have plotted relative annual changes in landings and price over the period for which data on both series are available (since 1980). It is clear that year-to-year

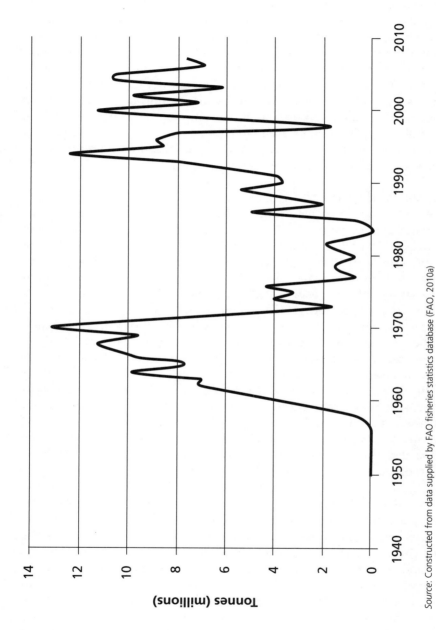

Source: Constructed from data supplied by FAO fisheries statistics database (FAO, 2010a)

Figure 1.4 *Landings from the Peruvian anchoveta fishery*

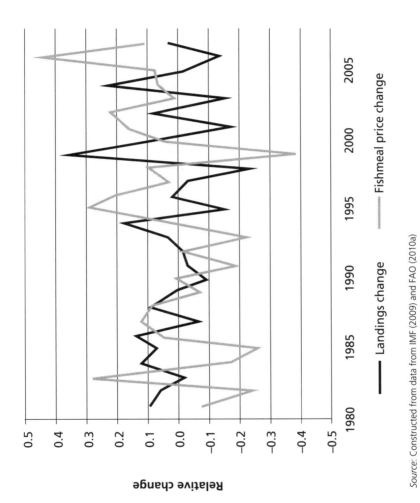

Source: Constructed from data from IMF (2009) and FAO (2010a)

Figure 1.5 *Fishmeal price and landings of herring, sardine and anchovy: relative annual changes*

changes in landings translate into price changes in the opposite direction: a fall in landings is associated with a rise in price, and vice versa. Fluctuations in supplies of these pelagics are thus quite quickly picked up by commodity markets, and the price effects will eventually be felt by all the downstream sectors, including consumers. What makes species such as anchoveta and menhaden economically important, therefore, is precisely this widespread range of effects which are felt when supplies change.

1.3.4 Are we facing a resource crisis?

The resource constraints which are now confronting capture fisheries raise a question over the maximum harvest levels that are attainable, both regionally and globally. A method for estimating the supply poten-tial of fisheries is discussed in more detail in Appendix A, but here we will focus on the constraints posed by stock depletion and over-exploita-tion, which have now become apparent in a number of important marine fisheries. In 2007, over one-quarter of world fish stocks were classed by the FAO as 'over-exploited, depleted or recovering'; roughly half were fully exploited, while only one-fifth were reckoned to be under-exploited or moderately exploited (FAO, 2009). The seriousness of the problem is the subject of much debate, though it is now recognized that fishing pres-sure not only reduces stock abundance, but may also put individual target species at risk of extinction or near-extinction (Pauly et al, 2002). One especially controversial paper, by Worm et al (2006), has predicted that on the basis of current trends, all commercial fisheries will collapse by 2048. However, this very bleak picture has since been modified some-what, and an assessment based on new evidence (or a more correct interpretation of the original data) suggests that the rate of exploitation is now declining and there are signs of recovery (Worm et al, 2009).

The severity of the resource crisis in particular sea areas, however, is quite striking. In the Atlantic, catches of cod have been on a downward trend since the late 1960s (Figure 1.6), with particularly sharp falls in the NW Atlantic in the early 1990s culminating in the collapse of the Newfoundland cod fishery in 1992. It is noteworthy that, despite the clo-sure of this fishery, landings of cod in this region have not recovered. While the decline in cod landings in both the NW and NE Atlantic has been due to catch restrictions on fishing vessels, arguably these have done no more than ratify the underlying problem of declining stock abundance. Direct evidence of stock depletion is illustrated most dra-matically in the case of North Sea cod: according to ICES data, cod spawning stock biomass fell over a 30-year period from 265,000 tonnes in 1971 to below 39,000 tonnes in 2006 (Figure 1.7). Stock levels reached an historic low in 2006, but have since shown signs of stabi-lization and recovery.

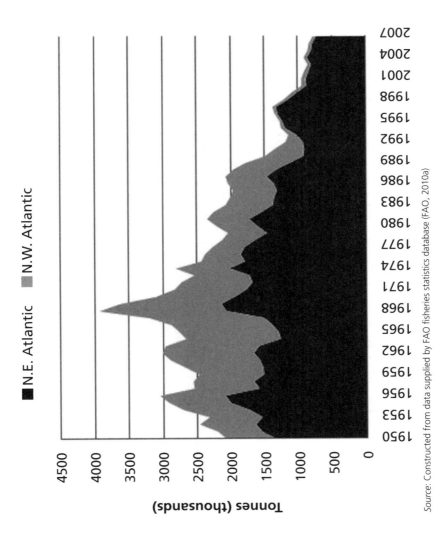

Figure 1.6 *Catches of Atlantic cod*

Source: Constructed from data supplied by FAO fisheries statistics database (FAO, 2010a)

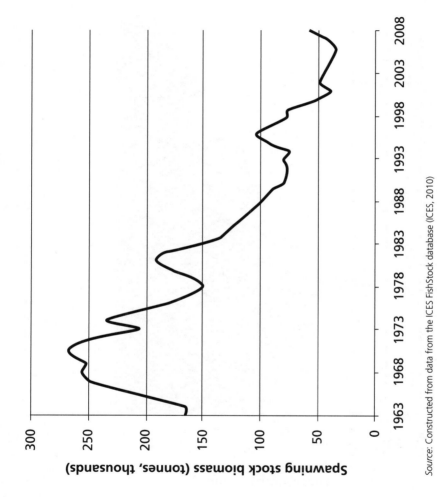

Figure 1.7 *North Sea cod: spawning stock biomass*

Source: Constructed from data from the ICES FishStock database (ICES, 2010)

Changes in status of world fish stocks have also had implications for the productivity of labour and capital employed in the fisheries sector. The slowdown in the rate of growth of global capture fisheries since the 1990s has seen catches rise at a more modest rate than in previous decades, in fact by just under 9 per cent over the 15 years from 1990 to 2005. Over the same period, however, the number of fishers employed increased more rapidly, by almost 43 per cent (FAO, 2008a), implying that average catch per fisher has fallen. This fall appears to have been most marked between 1995 and 2000 (Figure 1.8). (The reader should note, however, that changes in the seasonality of labour may make 'number of fishers' a less than perfect measure of labour input.) The significance of this in economic terms is that, in the absence of any compensating changes in other variables (e.g. fish prices), average returns per unit of labour will have fallen, with a direct impact on livelihoods. By contrast, labour productivity in aquaculture has risen over the same period, a reflection of the quite different conditions that operate in this sector compared with capture fisheries. Two distinguishing features of aquaculture are the ability to control the production process through husbandry, and the opportunity to establish ownership rights to the resource, both of which set it apart from capture fisheries, which largely remain a hunting activity and where the resource is res nullius (property of nobody) (Welcomme, 1996; Whitmarsh and Seijo, 2007; Asche and Bjorndal, 2010). A further contrast concerns the role of technological change, which in capture fisheries has been a contributory factor in overfishing, but which in aquaculture since 1950 has led to a threefold increase in the number of species that can be profitably farmed (World Bank, 2006).

This success has come at a price, however, since intensive aquaculture production systems have created significant environmental costs, including chemical and organic pollution, habitat destruction, saline intrusion into adjacent farmland, and the transmission of diseases and parasites to other species (Naylor et al, 1998; Black, 2001; Read and Fernandes, 2003; Anderson, 2007; Holmer et al, 2008). Moreover, aquaculture may arguably have worsened the resource crisis in capture fisheries through what is dubbed the 'fishmeal trap': that is, by intensifying the demand for fishmeal as a raw material in aquafeed, it has indirectly increased pressure on stocks such as anchoveta, sand eel and menhaden. While this may appear to cast doubt over the sustainability of aquaculture as a production system, the seriousness of the problem depends in large part on the effectiveness of the management regime imposed on the capture fishery. As Asche and Bjorndal (2010) have made clear, if controls on harvesting activity are working as they are supposed to do, increased demand for the targeted species cannot endanger the stock. It will, nonetheless, translate into higher prices for fishmeal

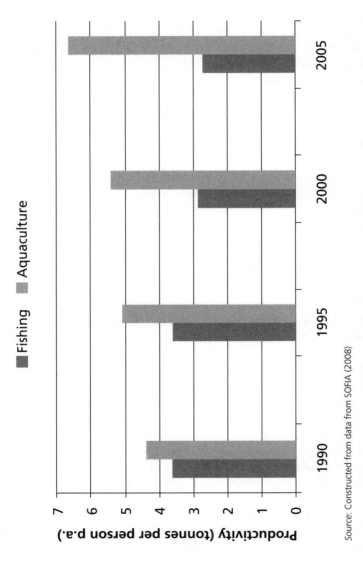

Source: Constructed from data from SOFIA (2008)

Figure 1.8 *Labour productivity in world capture fisheries and aquaculture*

and fish oil, which will in turn raise the price of farmed fish to an extent that will depend upon the economic feasibility of substituting lower-cost vegetable-based inputs into the diet. In the case of salmon farming, it appears that substitution has been occurring, since fishmeal input use per unit of fish output has been on the decline (Tveteras and Tveteras, 2010).

1.3.5 Climate change and its economic significance for fisheries

Future production from fisheries and aquaculture is expected to be strongly influenced by climate change, whose impact has already become apparent in a number of ways. There is evidence of a movement of fish towards the Poles in response to rising sea temperatures, increased frequency and severity of extreme events such as flooding, hydrological changes leading to the shrinkage of inland water bodies (e.g. Lake Chad), and the loss of critical habitat such as coral due to bleaching caused by warmer seas and acidification (Brander, 2007; FAO, 2008b). While it is difficult to judge whether the overall effect of climate change on capture fisheries will be positive or negative, it is clear that it will have important implications for livelihoods in particular sectors and regions. At the very least, the expected changes in the geographical distribution and abundance of target species will mean that onshore facilities, transport routes and fishing communities will become dislocated in relation to the natural resource. Daw et al (2009) cite the example of Pacific tuna, which is predicted to move north in response to sea temperature changes with the result that existing infrastructures that support the fishery will in future be disadvantaged by distance. The direct impact of climate change in aquaculture is expected to differ according to the zone of activity. De Silva and Soto (2009) suggest that fish farming carried out in temperate regions is likely to be negatively impacted, since increases in water temperature will adversely affect the growth rate of cold water species and also increase the risk of disease outbreaks. In tropical and subtropical climatic zones, by contrast, elevated water temperatures are expected to have a positive effect on production. Aside from these direct impacts, the culture of carnivorous species is likely to be indirectly affected if climate change reduces the raw material supplies from capture fisheries used in the manufacture of fishmeal and fish oil.

How vulnerable are national economies to climate-induced changes in fisheries? Vulnerability can be defined in this context as 'the susceptibility of groups or individuals to harm as a result of climatic changes' (Daw et al, 2009: p116), and is the central concept in an important study by Allison et al (2009) on the socio-economic significance of climate change on the capture fisheries of a cross-section of countries worldwide. The study constructs a vulnerability index composed of three elements that account for: the degree of exposure to the hazardous effects of climate change; the socio-economic dependence of a country on the fisheries sector; and the institutional capacity to respond to the climate change threat. The results for 132 countries revealed that vulnerability to climate change effects in fisheries was highest in regions located in West and Central Africa, north-west South America and parts of tropical Asia. The top quartile of the dataset (33 of the 132), representing the most vulnerable countries, included 22 from Africa. The real significance of these results is that vulnerable countries are generally much more dependent on fish as a source of dietary protein compared to other countries, and are also amongst the poorest. The disruption to fish supplies caused by climate change will thus produce the greatest hardship amongst precisely those communities where food security and poverty alleviation are already pressing issues (e.g. West Africa; see Figures 1.9 and 1.10).

1.4 Conclusion

The marine environment fulfils the important functions of providing society with natural resources for use in economic activity, and as a depository or sink for the resultant waste products. The way in which the economy interacts with the marine environment is crucial for its sustainability, and this is illustrated in the case of capture fisheries, which in recent years have levelled off and in many areas are showing clear signs of severe over-exploitation. The antecedents of the present problems may be traced to the very factors which initially drove the expansion for the first two decades of the post-WWII period, namely technological change in fish catching and processing, and increasing demand for fisheries products. In retrospect it is apparent, based on well-documented case studies of fisheries, that technical progress against a background of generally ineffective fisheries management has almost certainly contributed to the overfishing of many fish stocks. This has been worsened by subsidies, either explicit or implicit, which have kept catching capacity at unsustainably high levels. These trends have led to a number of quite pessimistic assessments of the prospects for world fisheries, unless remedial measures are taken.

A very different picture emerges when we look at the development of aquaculture, whose rapid expansion has made up for much of the shortfall in supplies from capture fisheries. Aquaculture is not without its own problems, however, and there are legitimate concerns about the environmental costs associated with particular farmed species (notably salmon and shrimp), and indeed about the sustainability of a global industry that places such heavy raw material demands on capture fisheries. It should be noted, however, that significant improvements have been made to some of these problematic sectors, specifically in the form

Figure 1.9 *Artisanal boat building in Sierra Leone*

Figure 1.10 *A selection of fish from an artisanal fishery in Sierra Leone*

of improved food conversion ratios (FCRs), substitution of vegetable in place of animal feeds and less intensive production methods. Climate change introduces a strong element of uncertainty into the picture, and while it may create new fishing opportunities as fish move to different sea areas, it is also likely to give rise to a range of hazards that will impact adversely on the catching and aquaculture sectors, both directly and indirectly. Looking to the future, there is a widely held belief that world demand for fisheries products is likely to outstrip supply, leading inevitably to a rise in prices in real terms, and this will have potentially serious consequences for food security in low-income food deficit countries (Kurien, 2005; Thorpe et al, 2007). These are the countries which are also the most vulnerable to climate-induced changes in their fisheries sectors, a problem made more serious where fish stocks are over-exploited and lack the resilience to withstand extreme events.

In the next chapter we look more closely at the resource constraints confronting the fisheries sector, and try to get to the roots of the over-fishing problem and how it can be resolved.

2
Overfishing and the Need for Management

2.1 Introduction

Economists attribute overfishing to the absence of property rights to the natural resource (i.e. the water body and the fish stock). A feature of many fisheries is that they are based on *common-pool resources*, which have two key characteristics that make them vulnerable to over-exploitation. These are:

(i) non-excludability – that is, it is difficult to exclude people from using them;
(ii) rivalry – that is, use by one person reduces availability for others.

Together, these characteristics have profoundly important consequences. To start with, there will be little incentive for any individual fishing firm to limit their harvesting activities, for to do so would simply mean leaving more of the resource to others exploiting the 'common pool'. As James Wilen explains, the insecurity of harvest entitlements distorts fishermen's behaviour in a way that compels them to compete wastefully (Wilen, 2006; see also Scott, 2008). Secondly, stock depletion caused by increasing fishing effort will manifest itself in lower catch rates for all participants, which means that fishing firms will then have to spend more time and money in order to harvest a given quantity of fish. To put the point another way, depletion of the common-pool resource implies that the average cost of catching a tonne of fish is raised. This state of affairs is an example of an *externality*, and is the key to understanding the economics of overfishing. Within the context of environmental economics, probably the best known example of an externality is climate change, which has been described as 'the mother of all externalities' (Tol, 2009).

2.2 A simple bioeconomic model to explain overfishing

We can develop these ideas more formally using a bioeconomic model, which is a system of relationships describing the interactions between the fish population and the harvesting activity of vessels. Bioeconomic modelling provides an analytical framework for examining:

- the effects on a fishery of changes on the supply side (e.g. caused by technical progress) and on the demand side (e.g. caused by advertising);
- the implications of different fisheries management strategies, particularly in respect of target reference points, such as open-access (OA), maximum sustainable yield (MSY) or maximum economic yield (MEY).

One of the simplest and most commonly used bioeconomic models is the Gordon-Schaefer (GS) model, which brings together the essential economic and biological elements of a fishery (Gordon, 1954; Schaefer, 1954, Clark, 1985; Cunningham et al, 1985; Bjorndal and Munro, 1998; Shah and Sharma, 2003). The regenerative properties of the natural resource are based on the assumption of logistic population growth, from which it is possible to show that a harvested fish stock will produce a sustainable yield (or surplus production) which will have a defined maximum. The economics of the model assumes that fishermen will be attracted into the fishery so long as there is profit to be made; whereas if losses are incurred, some will leave the fishery. Given assumptions about market price and the cost of fishing, it is possible to derive the level of fishing effort (= input) and yield (= output) that would be expected in the long run if there are no restrictions on entry and exit. This equilibrium state is termed *open-access*, and is one of the defining features of common-pool resources. In open-access, the fish stock has become sufficiently depleted that fishing is no longer profitable.

The basic argument can be developed diagrammatically, using hypothetical data for illustration (Table 2.1). For readers interested in the mathematics of the GS bioeconomic model, Appendix B outlines the main functional relationships and fisheries management reference points. We start with the sustainable yield curve, which describes the long-run relationship between fishing effort and harvestable output (Figure 2.1). This is a physical relationship, with effort measured in standardized units that reflect the catching power of the fleet (e.g. vessel horsepower-days) and output measured by weight of fish caught (e.g. kg). The curve is parabolic, and there is a unique effort level (E_{msy}) at which yield is maximized (maximum sustainable yield, or MSY). It is important to understand that the short-run catch–effort relationship may be quite different from this, and in practice it may appear that fishing vessels are able to catch much larger volumes of fish than are implied by Figure 2.1. The point is, however, that such high catches may be the result of not just the removal of the surplus production (i.e. growth), but the 'mining' of the standing stock. As such, the yield would not be truly sustainable, since catches would be likely to fall in subsequent periods as a consequence of stock depletion. Figure 2.1 is therefore describing the yield that can be obtained from a given effort level in biological equilibrium; that is, once the fish population has adjusted to the pressure of harvesting. It is also instructive to look at what happens to vessel catch rates as total fishing effort increases, and this is shown in Figure 2.2. The parabolic yield curve implies that the relationship between catch per unit of effort (CPUE) and effort will be linear and downward sloping, meaning that as more vessels enter a fishery, their average catch (physical productivity) declines. This is symptomatic of the fall in stock abundance, which is itself a consequence of intensified fishing.

Table 2.1 *The Gordon-Schaefer bioeconomic model: hypothetical data*

Effort	Yield	CPUE	Revenue 1	Revenue 2	Cost	Rent 1	Rent 2
0	0		0	0	0	0	0
5	47.5	9.5	950	1425	300	650	1125
10	90.0	9.0	1800	2700	600	1200	2100
15	127.5	8.5	2550	3825	900	1650	2925
20	160.0	8.0	3200	4800	1200	2000	3600
25	187.5	7.5	3750	5625	1500	2250	4125
30	210.0	7.0	4200	6300	1800	2400	4500
35	227.5	6.5	4550	6825	2100	2450	4725
40	240.0	6.0	4800	7200	2400	2400	4800
45	247.5	5.5	4950	7425	2700	2250	4725
50	250.0	5.0	5000	7500	3000	2000	4500
55	247.5	4.5	4950	7425	3300	1650	4125
60	240.0	4.0	4800	7200	3600	1200	3600
65	227.5	3.5	4550	6825	3900	650	2925
70	210.0	3.0	4200	6300	4200	0	2100
75	187.5	2.5	3750	5625	4500	−750	1125
80	160.0	2.0	3200	4800	4800	−1600	0
85	127.5	1.5	2550	3825	5100	−2550	−1275
90	90.0	1.0	1800	2700	5400	−3600	−2700
95	47.5	0.5	950	1425	5700	−4750	−4275
100	0	0	0	0	6000	−6000	−6000

Assumptions:
Unit cost of effort = 60 per day
Price for Revenue 1 = 20 per tonne
Price for Revenue 2 = 30 per tonne

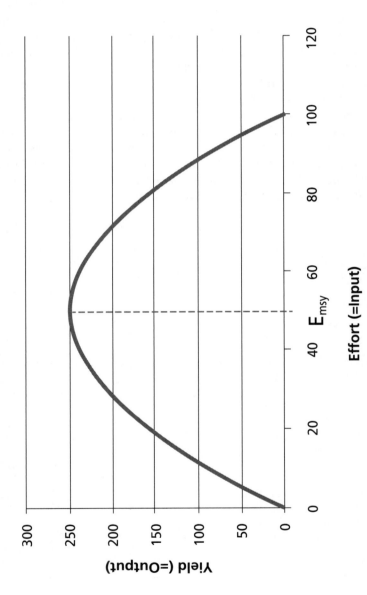

Figure 2.1 *Sustainable yield as a function of effort (GS model)*

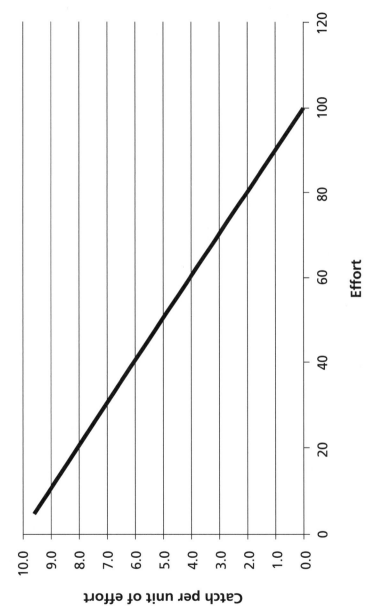

Figure 2.2 *Catch per unit of effort (CPUE) as a function of effort (GS model)*

How intensively a fishery will be exploited, and indeed whether it will be exploited commercially at all, is predicted by the model to depend on economic factors. For a given market price, the total money revenue that can be earned by selling the catch is shown in Figure 2.3. If the price is unaffected by the volume of fish landed, which is a reasonable assumption if the fishery in question is just a small part of a larger world market (e.g. tuna), then the shape of the revenue curve (R) will be identical to that of Figure 2.1, except that the units will be monetary (e.g. £, €, $), not physical (kg, lb). The level of effort that generates the most revenue corresponds with the MSY effort level, but to establish how much profit is earned, we need to have information about costs. If the total cost of fishing increases directly in proportion to fishing effort, we can superimpose a straight line graph (C) onto Figure 2.3 so as to compare it with total revenue (R). The intersection of these two functions defines the open-access level of fishing effort (E_{oa}). If effort is less than this, profits will be earned and effort will be attracted into the fishery, and vice versa. It needs to be stressed that the simple GS bioeconomic model that we are outlining here says nothing about the time horizon over which open access is reached, or the trajectory that a fishery will follow in practice as it moves towards equilibrium. Nonetheless, it provides an important benchmark against which to evaluate the performance of a fishery, and the underlying economic forces that drive its development. As shown in Figure 2.3, the position of the revenue and cost curves imply that the maximum sustainable yield (MSY) could be achieved with less effort than that predicted at open access. In purely physical terms, therefore, the fishery is over-exploited, since $E_{oa} > E_{msy}$.

Before going on to consider other reference points, it is useful to consider how the open-access equilibrium may change. In theory, anything that increases profitability will tend to encourage more effort into the fishery and increase pressure on the stocks. This might include a higher price of fish (e.g. due to rising demand) or lower harvesting costs (e.g. due to a fuel subsidy or more efficient capture methods). The reverse also applies, and indeed one of the ways in which effort may be reduced is by imposing a tax on catch or effort in order to reduce profitability. These regulatory options could be represented, respectively, by a downward shift in the total revenue curve, or an upward shift in the total cost curve. However, let us see how the fishery might be affected if market demand increased – for example, because of a successful advertising campaign – and the price that fishermen received for their catch rose as a result. As Figure 2.4 shows, the revenue curve is now 'stretched' so that the revenue that could potentially be earned at MSY is now higher. But the consequence of this is that the open-access equilibrium is disturbed, and specifically we anticipate that that effort will expand under the incentive of higher prices. This in turn will impact negatively on fish

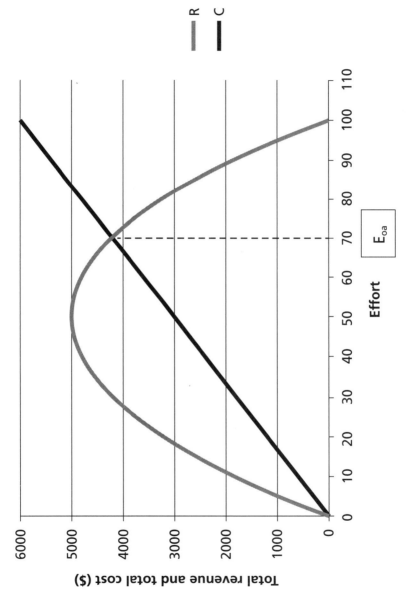

Figure 2.3 *Open-access equilibrium under initial price conditions*

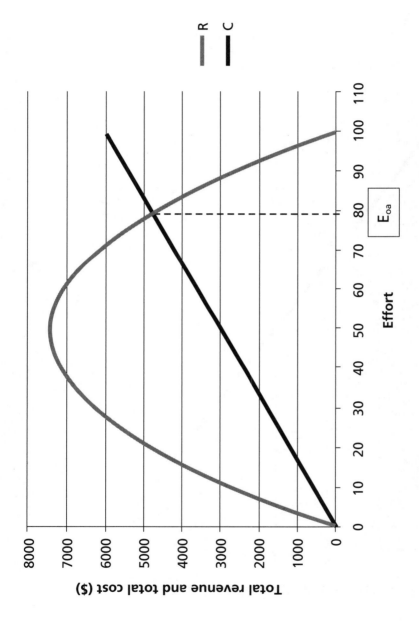

Figure 2.4 *Open-access equilibrium after increased demand*

stock biomass, but also, most crucially for the fishermen, the physical productivity of fishing as measured by CPUE. In the simple GS model we can show in theory that in economic terms there is an exact symmetry here, with the benefits of higher market price offset in the long run by lower CPUE.

There is another aspect to the overfishing problem, which is illustrated in Figure 2.5. This diagram corresponds to the situation before the market price of fish had been driven up by higher demand. For the moment, let us make the assumption that the cost of effort accurately reflects the real alternative use value of the inputs (i.e. the labour and capital) that are involved in fishing activity. In other words, if the total cost of effort in the fishery is €X, that is the value of what has to be sacrificed elsewhere in the economy in terms of forgone output. The difference between the value of the harvested fish (represented by R) and the real resource cost needed to produce it (represented by C) is the economic rent from the fishery. The level of effort at which economic rent is greatest is E_{mey}, which defines the maximum economic yield from the fishery. In the diagram, it is clear that the problem with open access is that it not only entails a sacrifice of fish (since catch at E_{oa} is less than E_{msy}), but a sacrifice of economic benefit (since economic rent is zero at E_{oa}). If the natural resource were controlled by a sole owner, whose objective was to maximize the economic return on his asset, then in theory harvesting would be limited to the E_{mey} level. But precisely because we are dealing with a common-pool resource, where property rights are poorly defined and access cannot be controlled, the economic rent is competed away. This situation is an example of what in economics is termed *market failure*, so called because the price mechanism fails to signal the true scarcity value of the natural resource (Hannesson, 1993). Rent that is lost in this way represents the real 'tragedy of the commons', since society is the poorer as a result. The trick, therefore, is somehow to prevent wasteful rent dissipation (in effect it gets invested in excessive catching capacity – 'overcapitalization') and to capture it in a socially useful way. In theory this might be achieved through taxes (see Appendix B), but in practice a range of control measures are commonly brought to bear. This is a policy issue, which we consider later. Meanwhile, let us return to the scenario we considered earlier in which the market price of fish has risen due to higher demand. We saw that in an open-access fishery this price-hike only succeeds in the long run in intensifying the pressure of fishing by attracting effort. However, as Figure 2.6 shows, it also implies that the economic rent that could potentially be earned at E_{mey} is greater since the output of the fishery is now more valuable.

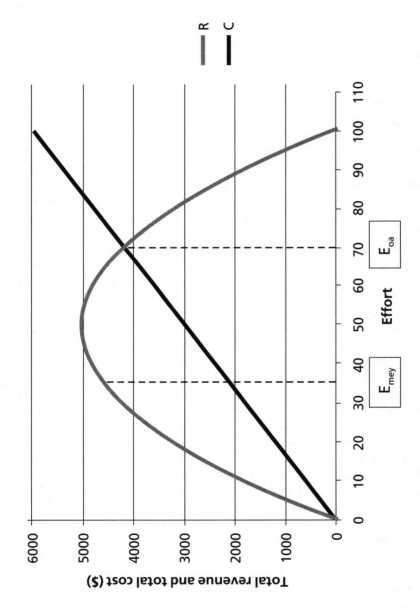

Figure 2.5 *Maximum economic yield under initial price conditions*

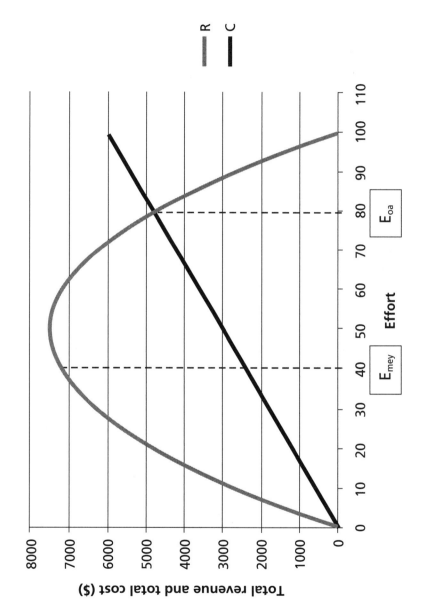

Figure 2.6 *Maximum economic yield after increased demand*

2.3 Estimating economic rent in practice

2.3.1 Limitations of surplus production models

Empirical studies of marine fisheries often involve bioeconomic models, and a common starting point for the simpler approaches is to estimate a surplus production model based on catch and effort data. This can then be used as the basis for deriving total revenue, given a knowledge of market prices, and if costs can be estimated it is possible to obtain at least a ballpark figure for economic rent. The advantage of surplus production models is that they can be used to estimate yield curves (and hence MSY) using only catch and effort data, but this in itself poses a number of problems that we can briefly outline.

To start with, vessels in a fleet typically differ in their fishing power, and a way must be found to standardize effort into a common unit of measurement (e.g. based on technical parameters such as hold capacity or engine size). The standardization problem is especially acute in developing countries, where coastal fisheries may be exploited by craft that range from simple row boats to much larger vessels with 600HP inboard diesel engines. A second measurement problem concerns the catch, and a characteristic of many artisanal fisheries is that a very wide variety of species are commonly landed. Studies of the small-scale fisheries in NW Sicily, for example, found that over 40 species of locally caught fish made up the catch of trammel-net fishermen (Pipitone et al, 2000). Aggregation by weight is the simplest way round this difficulty, but if the catch composition is changing over time then this raises questions about the underlying biology of the surplus production model that we are trying to identify. Thirdly, there is a statistical problem stemming from the fact that a fishery described by the catch and effort data will almost certainly not be in equilibrium. Indeed, in a rapidly expanding fishery the observations will probably lie above the 'true' yield curve, since catches will consist not just of the sustainable yield (= surplus production), but also part of the standing stock of fish. As such, the result may give an over-optimistic picture of the state of exploited fish stocks, carrying the clear risk that management authorities may permit too high a level of fishing effort. Recent years have seen a number of suggestions for minimizing the 'equilibrium problem', and the method we adopt in the following example is based on one of these more modern fitting procedures. The final problem relates to the shape of the yield curve itself. In the previous section we developed the bioeconomic model on the assumption of a parabolic yield curve (as summarized in Appendix B), but many empirical studies of fisheries have shown that a better 'fit' to the data is obtained using a different mathematical specification. One of the best known of these is the non-symmetric yield curve initially developed by Fox (1970), and the example that follows is based on a version of this approach. The broader point at issue, however, is that deciding on the best model for a fishery in practice may need to be made on statistical as well as *a priori* grounds.

2.3.2 Case study

The example considered here is based on a study by Sinan and Whitmarsh (2010) of the marine fisheries in the Maldives, an island republic in the Indian Ocean. Catches are dominated by tuna species, with skipjack (*Katsuwonus pelamis*) currently constituting some 70 per cent of the total. The relevant catch and effort data are presented in Table 2.2, and show a threefold increase in total landings over a 20-year period since the mid-1980s. The figures relate to the fishing activity of local vessels operating within the Coastal Fishery Zone (CFZ), and constitute almost the whole of reported landings. In the original paper, the catch and effort data were used to estimate two alternative models of the fishery, one a 'threshold'-type relationship (whose main property is that catch increases with effort, but levels out so as to approach its maximum asymptotically) and the other a surplus production model based on the method developed by Clarke et al (1992). Below we present the results of the second of these models, the main elements of which are given in Appendix C.

Figure 2.7 presents the fitted yield curve with the actual catch-effort data points superimposed. Sustainable yield is maximized at just over 150,000 tonnes, requiring an effort of 377,000 vessel-trips. Interestingly, the pattern of observations reveals that the highest effort actually attained in the fisheries was below 300,000 day trips (in the year 2007 – see Table 2.2), which is less than the calculated E_{msy}. In other words, there are no obvious signs of biological overfishing. However, this tells us nothing about the economic performance of the fisheries, for which we require additional data in order to derive the appropriate revenue and cost functions. To value catch, an estimate of $1314 per tonne is used, based on the market prices of the main species landed. To monetize effort, a figure calculated from a cost and earnings survey of $632 per vessel-trip is employed. When we graph out the revenue and cost curves for the fishery, we obtain Figure 2.7. The effort level predicted to occur at open access is just over 306,000 vessel-trips, while the corresponding figure for MEY is slightly below 137,000 trips. The economic rent that can be generated from the fishery at E_{mey} is represented by the vertical distance between the revenue and cost curves, which Sinan and Whitmarsh (2010) calculate to be $49 million per annum. Since the fishery is believed to be operating under *de facto* open-access conditions, which seems plausible since the configuration of data points in Figure 2.7 corresponds quite closely with the predicted E_{oa} shown in Figure 2.8, it is reasonable to assume that this economic rent is lost. To put this

Table 2.2 *Maldivian fisheries: effort, catch and CPUE*

Year	Effort Vessel day-trips (thousands)	Catch Tonnes (thousands)	CPUE Tonnes per trip
1985	93.6	61.4	0.656
1986	91.1	58.9	0.646
1987	82.8	56.6	0.684
1988	80.1	71.3	0.890
1989	71.1	70.7	0.994
1990	78.2	76.4	0.977
1991	82.5	80.6	0.977
1992	88.2	81.8	0.928
1993	99.8	89.7	0.899
1994	111.5	104.0	0.933
1995	128.2	104.6	0.816
1996	139.8	105.4	0.754
1997	156.7	101.8	0.649
1998	164.8	115.1	0.699
1999	177.0	123.3	0.696
2000	199.9	115.4	0.577
2001	233.1	125.0	0.536
2002	262.9	160.2	0.610
2003	275.9	152.2	0.552
2004	285.6	155.6	0.545
2005	277.5	182.9	0.659
2006	266.7	181.0	0.679
2007	298.4	141.1	0.473

Source: Sinan and Whitmarsh (2010)

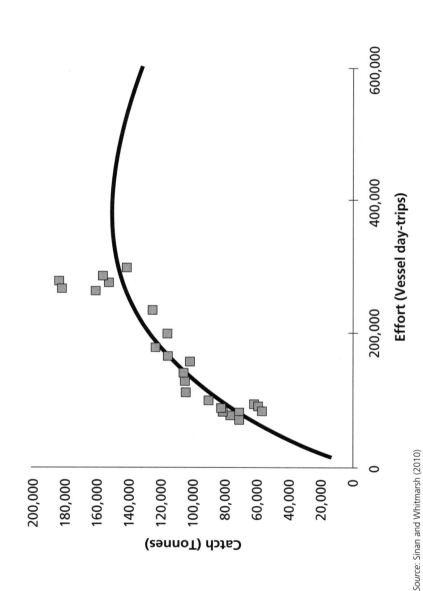

Source: Sinan and Whitmarsh (2010)

Figure 2.7 *Catch and effort in the Maldivian fisheries: actual observations and fitted yield curve*

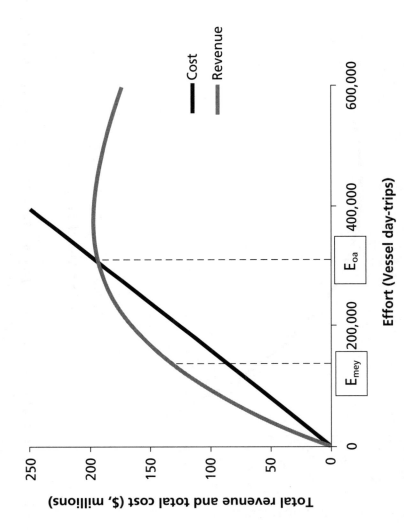

Source: Sinan and Whitmarsh (2010)

Figure 2.8 *Fitted revenue and cost curves in the Maldivian fisheries*

figure into perspective, the total revenue from the Maldivian fisheries in the most recent year (2007) was some $185 million dollars, so the forgone rent represents over one-quarter of this value.

2.4 Tackling the overfishing problem

2.4.1 The rationale for management

The bioeconomic model as described here is obviously a very simplified representation of a complex situation, but it nevertheless provides a coherent explanation as to the causes of overfishing and what society stands to lose in consequence. It is worth noting the global scale of the problem. In what will surely become a landmark study, a report by the World Bank and the UN Food and Agriculture Organization (FAO) estimated the loss of economic rent from sea fisheries worldwide to be in the order of $50 billion per year (World Bank, 2009). The report emphasizes the significance of this loss by drawing attention to the link between fisheries and other sectors, since forgone economic rent implies that capital investment projects elsewhere in the economy are denied funds. A similar point is made by Cunningham and Neiland (2005), who highlight the magnitude of the losses from fisheries by suggesting that as a rule-of-thumb, the forgone rents represent somewhere between 30 per cent and 60 per cent of turnover (total sales revenue). Possibly the most fundamental aspect of the bioeconomic model, however, is that it implies that the overfishing problem is not self-correcting. Earlier we used the term 'market failure' to describe the situation in which the true value of the natural resource is not reflected in the price that fishermen pay for access, and so long as that state of affairs lasts, the rent drain will in theory continue for eternity. This argument would seem to provide a fairly compelling rationale for fisheries to be regulated and managed, in order to tackle the problem of over-exploitation. To be sure, the topic of fisheries management is large and complex, and it is not the aim of this book to give a detailed account of the many different institutional arrangements that have developed in practice. Nonetheless, it is important to distil some lessons from the experience of fisheries management, and a necessary starting point is to outline the methods that are commonly used to regulate fishing activity, and some of their pros and cons.

2.4.2 Fisheries management control measures

Table 2.3 presents a typology of measures, where it will be seen that a basic distinction is drawn between those which rely on administrative controls on fishing activity, and those which make use of economic instruments involving either fishermen or consumers. We consider each in turn:

Table 2.3 *A typology of fisheries management control measures*

Approach	Measure	Examples and mode of operation
Administrative controls	Output controls	Total allowable catches (TACs), allocated nationally and/or at community and sector level.
	Input controls	Limits on total fleet capacity via licensing; effort controls on individual vessels (e.g. days at sea, size and engine power).
	Area-based measures	Exclusion zones applied to some or all vessels (possibly as part of a marine reserve prohibiting other activities).
	Non area-based measures	Technical conservation measures (e.g. mesh regulations, gear bans, minimum landing sizes, closed seasons, by-catch limits).
Economic instruments	User rights	Individual transferable quotas (ITQs) or effort entitlements awarded to fishermen; territorial user rights (TURFs) assigned at community level.
	Access payments	Charges imposed on effort (e.g. licence fees) or on catch (e.g. royalties on quantity landed).
	Price controls	Controls on prices paid (e.g. by a monopoly state purchasing agency) to fishermen for landed fish.
	Demand-side measures	Ecolabelling and seafood certification; consumer awareness campaigns; environmental scoring and 'traffic light' sustainability systems.

(i) Administrative controls

Administrative controls typically restrict the quantity of fish that can be harvested, the conditions under which the fish can be taken (landing size, season, area), the number of vessels or their total catching capacity, the effort that each vessel can exert, the technical configuration of the fleet, and the capture methods that are permitted to be used. Such measures, which have a long history of use in fisheries management, represent what might be termed the 'command and control' approach to regulation. The problem with administrative controls is that, as one astute observer has remarked, one ends up administering everything. What tends to happen is that, as each set of measures is found to be deficient, the management authorities feel compelled to add a further layer of controls on top of those already there. A more fundamental problem, and arguably the reason why administrative controls so often seem to be weak or ineffective, is that fishermen have shown themselves to be remarkably adept at getting round them. This result is perfectly consistent with economic behaviour, and as such entirely predictable. In the UK, for example, the relatively lax controls on fishing vessels of below 10m in length resulted in a growing proportion of vessels in the fleet below this size threshold (Whitmarsh, 1997). There is also plenty of anecdotal evidence testifying to the willingness of fishermen to have their vessels altered in order to take advantage of the current regulations. Where quotas are allocated according to vessel size, it is not unknown for undersized boats to be 'stretched' by a few feet, so as to put them into a higher length category and thus to qualify for a greater catch entitlement.

The problems associated with some of the more traditional types of administrative control, particularly technical conservation measures and effort restrictions, have seen a shift of emphasis towards area-based management in the form of partial or total fisheries exclusion zones. This move parallels the growing interest in the use of marine protected areas (MPAs), of which there are an increasing number worldwide. MPAs establish rules that aim to reduce the effect of human activity (including fishing) on key ecosystem variables. MPAs are also seen as having an important role in ecosystem approaches to fisheries management (EAF), and specifically those aspects of the process that focus on the biophysical components of the ecosystem (FAO, 2003). The evidence suggests that MPAs offer a number of specific benefits that include: reduced risk of stock collapse, increased sustainable yields (via biomass export), protection of vulnerable habitats, and the maintenance of species biodiversity (Sanchirico, 2000; Sanchirico et al, 2002). However, whether these effects are sufficient to justify the permanent establishment of marine exclusion zones (MEZs) on economic efficiency criteria is not clear. While it is acknowledged that exclusion zones may mitigate the worst effects of over-exploitation, on their own they do nothing to solve the open-access problem in the sea areas that are unrestricted. Indeed, MPAs have been described as one of a number of 'blunt instruments' being adopted to deal with the fisheries problem (Cunningham et al, 2009), and their use can be regarded as tacit admission that traditional management approaches have failed. Accordingly, it is difficult to see how the use of MPAs, in the absence of other measures, can prevent economic rent in the fishery from being dissipated. MPAs are certainly not a panacea, though they may possibly be part of the solution.

(ii) Economic instruments

Economic instruments avoid many of the distortions associated with administrative controls, though experience suggests that they are not without problems. On the positive side, economic instruments in the form of user rights, such as individual quotas (IQs), have been shown to be an effective way of rationalizing fishing fleets and removing excess capacity. In combination with access payments, they can also be used to appropriate the economic rent from a fishery, as has been demonstrated in the case of Namibian hake, where quota fees have enabled the government to recover at least part of the available rent from this very valuable resource (Manning, 2005). Individual quotas may be transferable or non-transferable, and several countries (e.g. New Zealand, Iceland) have made individual transferable quotas (ITQs) the cornerstone of their fisheries management regimes. ITQs typically work by giving fishing firms an entitlement to catch a specified quantity (i.e. x tonnes per year) or a share of the total quota, which can then be traded. It is the process of trading which brings about rationalization, as firms which relinquish their rights are obliged to exit the fishery. However, relying on market forces alone to allocate user rights will result inevitably in a concentration not just of ownership, but also of wealth, since the rights will come to command an economic value through buying and selling. If the outcome is that already poor fishermen end up without any entitlements to the resource, this may be considered socially unacceptable.

Charges can be used to appropriate the economic rent from a fishery, either on their own or in combination with a system of user rights, and indeed are a common method of regulating the activities of foreign vessels operating in the waters of coastal state fishing nations. The experience of fishing access agreements, however, suggests that they often face a number of difficulties. In principle, they are a good way in which a host country that lacks the domestic catching capacity can take advantage of its fisheries resources by effectively 'buying in' the harvesting services of a distant water fishing nation (DWFN). In practice, there is strong evidence that access conditions are often loaded heavily in favour of DWFNs, who typically pay a very low proportion of the value of the catch in the form of fees to the host country (ICTSD, 2006). If that is true, it means that coastal states – which in the majority of fishing access agreements are developing countries – may only be capturing a fraction of the potential rents from their marine resources. An alternative mechanism for imposing what is, in effect, a tax on fishing, is where fishermen are required to sell their catch at a set price to a state agency, which then markets it at higher prices for export. This system was used in Mauritania and the Maldives for a number of years (Valatin, 2000), though in the latter country was later discontinued despite its having been an effective way of collecting economic rent and controlling effort (Sathiendrakumar and Tisdell, 1997). In Mauritania, the role and function of the fish-trading company (SMCP) has changed over time, and its effectiveness as a resource rent generator seems to have been attenuated; it has nevertheless made a positive contribution to the process of fisheries management and proved an effective instrument of tax collection (Cunningham et al, 2005).

A novel and quite radical application of economic instruments involves demand-side measures for raising consumer awareness of the environmental attributes of fisheries products, in order to influence their purchasing decisions. The best known example of this is the scheme operated by the Marine Stewardship Council (MSC), under which seafood products originating from fisheries that are certified as being 'sustainable and well-managed' are awarded an ecolabel. Such recognition is expected to translate into market benefits, enabling a price premium to be charged for certified products bearing the MSC logo, since consumers who are concerned about the environment are willing to pay more for the ecolabelled product. The scheme is thus intended to promote and incentivize good fisheries management practice by the prospect of higher market returns.

The point to note about demand-side measures of this kind, however, is that they are only as effective as the supply-side controls on which they are predicated. If these prove weak and ineffective in the face of increased demand, and fishing pressure is not contained, the long-term benefits are hardly likely to be durable. Indeed, complementary demand-side measures such as ecolabelling make the need to solve the open-access problem more imperative, not less. Provided that condition is satisfied, however, the demand-side approach seems at least to offer the hope that fishermen themselves have something to gain from cooperating with the fisheries management process.

2.4.3 The complexity of management

The history of fisheries management has, to a large extent, been one of trial and error. This should come as no surprise, given the complexity of the systems, human and ecological, that we are attempting to manage.

Moreover, the wider experience of dealing with the problems of common-pool resources suggests that a 'one size fits all' solution is unlikely to be found; as Ostrom (2008) has noted, the institutional arrangements that work well in one particular situation may fail in others. But to understand why the management of fisheries has proved so problematic, we need to consider the political context in which decisions are made. In practice, fisheries managers will typically have several objectives (biological, economic, social) which may be incompatible and which cannot all be simultaneously achieved. Managers might aim, therefore, for a compromise in which no single objective is maximized, but the worst outcome for each is avoided and the fewest number of people complain – a strategy described entertainingly by John Pope as 'minimum sustainable whinge' (Pope, 1997). Adding to the problem is what Charles (1992) has referred to as the 'natural tensions' between different world views of the ultimate purpose of fisheries management, reflecting deep divisions over the priority that should be accorded to three main areas: conservation and the protection of fish stocks; economic efficiency and wealth generation; and the maintenance of maritime communities. These three opposing paradigms, it is contended, have their counterpart in the types of management measures that are prescribed. The complexity of the decision-making is further compounded where, as is increasingly the case with all marine resources, policy-makers need to look beyond sectoral interests and consider fisheries within the wider framework of coastal zone management. The creation of marine protected areas (MPAs) is a good example of this kind of issue, since MPAs almost of necessity impinge on a range of human activities (recreation, shipping, marine aggregates, fisheries, aquaculture, etc.) and involve multiple stakeholder groups.

2.5 Conclusions

A short anecdote may help encapsulate some of the ideas presented in this chapter. Asked at a meeting whether regulation of his local fishing industry would be a good idea, one of the top trawler owners was quick to dismiss the idea, on the grounds that 'economics would sort it out'. He meant, presumably, supply and demand would allow the better operators to outperform the weaker ones. To that extent he was perfectly correct, but it was pointed out to him that unfortunately in open-access fisheries, market forces typically 'sort it out' in another way altogether. Indeed, it is nearly always possible to find fisheries where some fishermen make a successful living, but that in itself tells us nothing about overall economic performance. For that we need a wider set of indicators, and when we look at these we are very often led to the conclusion that a fisheries management strategy of some kind is required.

Bieoconomic analysis helps explain why overfishing occurs, but it also draws attention to what society stands to lose as a result. Over-exploitation of marine fisheries ultimately impacts (adversely) on all stakeholders: fishermen, processors, consumers, taxpayers. The experience of fisheries management has shown that overfishing has proved difficult to solve, and the measures to deal with it have typically been unsuccessful, since they have tended to treat the symptoms rather than the causes. A corollary of this is that the costs of fisheries management can be substantial and, where these are not matched by economic benefits, it raises questions over the efficiency of the management process itself (Arnason et al, 2000). Failure to tackle the overfishing problem is especially serious for developing countries, not only because it may jeopardize food security directly, but because it deprives the economy of a key source of wealth in the form of economic rent (Cunningham et al, 2009). Yet despite its dismal track record, fisheries management can be successful so long as the political will is there and the cause of the problem is correctly diagnosed. Experience with economic instruments (e.g. rights-based governance in the form of user rights and access payments) has been generally positive, and the future may well see this approach combined with spatially differentiated management in the form of MPAs.

3
Collecting and Using
Socio-economic Data on Fisheries

3.1 Introduction

So far, we have said nothing about how socio-economic data about marine living resources is obtained in practice, but this is clearly essential if key questions regarding their use and development are to be answered. The purpose of such data is not merely to present an up-to-date picture of the current economic status of marine resources, but to see how their status might change in the immediate future (e.g. as a consequence of intervention, and what the implications will be for different stakeholder groups and for society as a whole. In policy terms, the issue is therefore not simply 'Where are we now?', but 'Where will we be if no action is taken?', and 'Where could we be if appropriate measures are imposed?'. The data collection challenge, especially as regards artisanal fisheries, is most pronounced in developing countries, where this sector is relatively large but geographically quite dispersed.

Information about fisheries is used by different groups to address a potentially wide range of questions. These comprise:

- fisheries managers (e.g. economic effects of control measures);
- finance authorities (e.g. tax implications of fisheries policy);
- fishermen (e.g. comparative operating performance);
- onshore sector (e.g. consumer response to product labelling);
- local government (e.g. job creation from recreational fishing trips);
- environmental agencies (e.g. conservation value of no-take fishing zones).

3.2 Data needs and sources

The main categories of socio-economic information on fisheries are summarized in Table 3.1, with an explanation of their purpose and policy relevance. It will be noticed that economic efficiency, which was the theme of the previous chapter, is but one of the issues that are likely to interest decision-makers who in practice need to obtain information on other areas (e.g. income and livelihoods, food security, trade perform-ance). This is certainly true of developing countries, where these issues are often of dominant political concern. Moreover, the theme of eco-nomic efficiency is itself more broadly defined than in our earlier discussion of resource rent and wealth maximization, and includes the idea that fishing may have adverse spillover effects ('negative externali-ties') which impose economic costs on other sectors. Pollution and environmentally destructive fishing methods come into this category. Obtaining data on such externalities is in practice extremely challenging, but is nonetheless important if the fisheries sector is to be optimally managed.

Table 3.1 *Socio-economic information on fisheries*

Information category	Purpose	Policy relevance (examples)
Income and livelihoods	To assess the well-being and living standards of fishers and fishing-dependent communities.	Financial hardship may justify favourable tax treatment or legislative changes affecting working conditions in the fishing industry.
Food security	To assess the availability of fish supplies to consumers and the dependence on fish in the diet.	Low or falling per capita fish consumption in food deficit countries may signify problems in the supply and distribution chain.
Trade performance	To assess the ability of the fisheries sector to generate foreign exchange and/or replace imports.	Falling export earnings from seafood, or increasing import penetration, may be due to currency overvaluation or supply-side problems in the fisheries sector.
Economic efficiency	To assess the socially optimal allocation of resources to the fishing sector and the effectiveness of their use.	Zero economic rent and/or low productivity may be symptomatic of over-exploitation, requiring effort control.

Let us now consider exactly what information needs to be obtained, and how it may be used. Specific variables that relate to the performance of the fisheries sector include:

- quantity of landings, by species;
- fishing effort and days at sea;
- vessel characteristics;
- fleet nationality;
- area and dates fished;
- labour and capital employed;
- prices of main species;
- operating costs of fishing;
- TACs and quotas, by species;
- exports and imports;
- per capita fish consumption;
- financial transfers and fisheries management costs.

Other indicators (e.g. financial surplus, resource rent, fleet capacity, quota uptake, trade balance, labour and capital productivity) may be derived from these elements.

In the first instance, these data may be collected purely to give a profile of the fisheries sector in terms of a number of indicators. However, policy-makers and managers are also interested in finding out about the role and significance of the fisheries sector in the economy as a whole, and this requires rather more data than the list just presented. To give an illustration, if we are concerned with food security and wish to assess the dependence on fish in the diet, it is often more meaningful to use a relative measure such as the percentage of fish in total animal protein intake. As such, we need information on food intake generally and not just on fish consumption. To take another example, in order to correctly account for changes over time in a monetary variable such as fishing income, we need to see how far it has risen or fallen in real terms relative to other sectors. In economics there is a standard procedure for doing this which requires us to 'deflate' the income series using a measure of underlying inflation in the economy as a whole (see Table 3.2). Where such data is lacking, or incomplete, the question cannot be answered. In fact, the need to transform data in this way is essential where we are trying to explain the causes of change in economic variables. In a similar way, in order to explain patterns of fish consumption, it is helpful to know the prices consumers have paid, since economic theory tells us that price is a determinant of demand. But it is real (not actual, or nominal) prices that count, and to calculate these requires a price deflator. The point, therefore, is that we require information not just about the fisheries sector alone, but about the economy of which it is a component part.

Table 3.2 *Nominal and real expenditure on fish by UK households*

Date	Fish expenditure	Fish expenditure Index (nominal)	Consumer Price Index	Fish expenditure index (real)
	Pence per person per week	Year 1987 = 100	Year 1987 = 100	Year 1987 = 100
1987	54.1	100.0	100.0	100.0
1997	77.2	142.6	147.8	96.5
2007	115.5	213.5	172.5	123.8

Notes:
The Consumer Price Index (CPI) is a measure of inflation in the economy, and is here used as a deflator to convert expenditure on fish from nominal to 'real' terms. The relationship is:

Real expenditure index = (Nominal expenditure index × 100)/CPI

This shows that over the 20 years, nominal household expenditure on fish more than doubled in the UK, but in real terms the rise was less than 25 per cent.

Sources:
(i) Expenditure data are derived from the DEFRA Family Food Survey, available at:
http://statistics.defra.gov.uk/esg
(ii) CPI data are derived from the IMF World Economic Outlook database, available at:
www.imf.org/external/pubs/ft/weo

Some of the data may be derived from publicly available sources, most of which are now accessible electronically. Online information relating to global capture fisheries and aquaculture production is supplied by the FAO Fisheries Information Global System (FIGIS) database (www.fao.org/fi/figis), which also includes commodity statistics on fisheries exports and imports in quantity and value terms. A good source of food consumption data covering a range of product groups and items, including fish and seafood, for countries worldwide is available from the FAO Food Security database (www.fao.org/economic/ess/food-security-statistics/en/). Detailed reported landings data for area-defined fish species in the North Atlantic are available from ICES (www.ices.dk), along with associated data on recruitment, fishing mortality, total and spawning stock biomass. Though the latter is presented in the first instance as biological information on the state of the stocks, some variables can still be of use in economic analysis. For example, trends in fishing mortality may be interpreted alongside fishing effort data (e.g. standard effort days) to account for the exploitation of a fishery, and stock biomass estimates may be incorporated into bioeconomic models for use in fisheries management. Fishing fleet statistics are fairly patchy, and for many countries no reliable data are available. The exception is Europe, where the Fleet Register (http://ec.europa.eu/fisheries/fleet/) allows users to track trends in EU vessel numbers and catching capacity, measured in tonnage and engine power. Aquaculture is being increasingly well documented through a number of websites (e.g. Aquamedia, at www.aquamedia.org), and it is now possible to obtain value and price data for the main farmed species, at least within Europe. International commodity prices for fishmeal of various grades are obtainable from the IMF World Economic Outlook database (www.imf.org/external/pubs/ft/weo).

For most detailed socio-economic assessments of fisheries, however, it is nearly always necessary to supplement these secondary sources with primary data collected using survey-based methods. The focus of these is usually on the following areas:

- financial and economic performance (e.g. costs and earnings of fishermen, fish farmers or traders);
- markets and prices (e.g. quayside quantities sold and prices received; household fish consumption and expenditure);
- attitudes and motivation (e.g. fishermen's view of prospects; consumer attitudes towards ecolabelled seafood).

Before looking at examples of these types of survey, let us review some of the basic steps that need to be followed and the pitfalls that are commonly encountered. At a fairly early stage, researchers need to define the sampling frame (i.e. the listing of all cases in the population from which the sample is drawn), and decide whether to adopt probability or nonprobability sampling. If a cost and earnings survey is being conducted, the sampling frame may comprise a list of vessel owners. The sample itself may appropriately be segmented (e.g. on the basis of vessel size, technology, area fished, metier, etc.) in order to ensure representative coverage of the fleet. The survey instrument would consist of a questionnaire, which may either be self-administered (e.g. by mail, delivery/collection or online) or interviewer administered (e.g. by phone or face-to-face). There are quite clear advantages and disadvantages to each of these methods, and the very low response rates commonly encountered using mailed-out questionnaires may leave face-to-face interviews as the only practical option (Anderson et al, 2008). Postal surveys, on the other hand, enjoy the benefit of being able to reach a geographically dispersed sample relatively cheaply, and this is a major consideration where a study (e.g. of public attitudes) is being investigated at national level. One particular problem encountered in artisanal fisheries is the lack of records, and it is often not feasible to conduct economic surveys which request data covering (say) the previous financial year. In these circumstances a record-keeping approach, in which selected participants are asked to keep a daily account of their fishing and trading activities, may be the preferred or indeed the only alternative (Pomeroy, 1992).

3.3 Cost and earnings studies

Cost and earnings studies of commercial fisheries aim to derive various measures of financial and economic surplus, and are usually conducted at the level of a representative individual vessel. The approach taken varies according to the purpose, though a common starting point is to use recognized accounting categories from which to distil a 'bottom line' figure. This is normally sufficient if we are concerned with fisher income, though if we want to find out whether the labour and capital have been used efficiently, we would need to go further and see what these resources could have earned in the next best alternative use (i.e. their opportunity cost). Routinely conducted cost and earnings studies can be useful for tracking the operating performance of a fishing fleet, and in fishery-dependent communities they are arguably essential for monitoring the degree of financial hardship. In addition to this, however, the raw data they supply can be used in investment appraisal of fisheries projects as well as economic modelling. We have already seen one example of this in the previous chapter, where the cost estimates from a fishing survey undertaken in the Maldives were used in a bioeconomic analysis of the fisheries in order to estimate maximum economic yield. In parallel with this, cost and earnings data can be used to answer a number of 'what-if?' questions concerning the financial impact of changes in key variables such as prices or catch rates. This is the focus of the present section.

The structure of a typical cost and earnings study is presented in Table 3.3, based on data from a sample of artisanal fishing vessels operating in the Mediterranean in the late 1990s. The vessels use trammel-gill

Table 3.3 *Cost and earnings data for a representative Mediterranean artisanal fishing vessel*

Item	Amount (€)	Per cent total revenue
Total revenue	10,837	100.0
Running costs (e.g. fuel costs)	1020	9.4
Fixed costs: nets and ropes	1705	15.7
Fixed costs: other	1597	14.7
Crew payments	3799	35.1
Total costs	8121	74.9
Net revenue	9817	90.6
Boat income	2716	25.1

Notes:
(i) The figures are based on the average performance of a sample of trammel-gill net vessels.
(ii) Running costs are proportional to vessel utilization rate and include fuel, ice, bait and other expenses.
(iii) Vessel fixed costs are incurred regardless of the amount of fishing activity. Apart from nets and ropes, fixed costs include repairs, maintenance, insurance and other items.
(iv) Net revenue is defined as total revenue minus running costs.
(v) Boat income is total revenue minus total costs.
Source: Unpublished data

nets to catch mostly high-value species such as red mullet, sea bream and hake. The crew on each boat comprises a skipper-owner plus one additional crewman who is paid a share of the value of the catch, this being a common arrangement in many types of small-scale fishery. Two measures of financial surplus are given, net revenue (excess over running costs) and boat income (excess over total costs). Taking the data as representative of the group, we can see that net revenue constituted on average 90 per cent and boat income 25 per cent of total revenue.

Consider now how the performance of this representative vessel would change if there were to be a change in catching opportunities. Specifically, let us see how net revenue and boat income would be impacted if catch rates were to deviate from their baseline level by a given amount. Using a short-run forecasting model (Whitmarsh et al, 2000), we start with the basic identity:

Boat income = Total revenue
minus running costs
minus vessel fixed costs
minus crew payments

We may express this as:

$$\pi = pUE - cE - F - w(pUE - cE)$$

where:

π = average boat income
p = price
U = vessel catch rate
c = unit running costs
E = vessel utilization
w = crew share rate
F = vessel fixed costs

For our representative artisanal fishing vessel, we have the following parameter values:

p = €7.83 per kg of fish landed
U = 7.134kg per day fishing
c = €5.256 per day fishing
E = 194 days fishing per year
w = 0.387 proportion of net revenue
F = €3302 per year

Figure 3.1 shows the effect of catch rate on the financial performance of the vessel. This is constructed on the *ceteris paribus* assumption that the

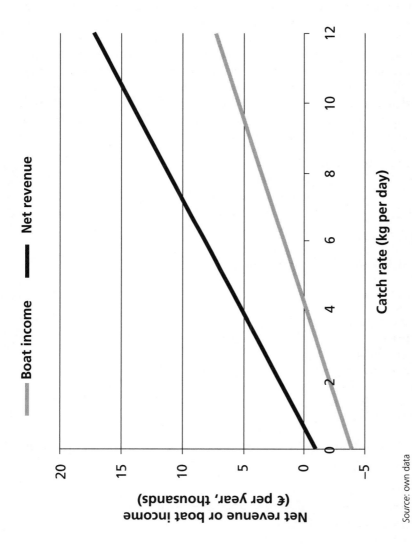

Source: own data

Figure 3.1 *Effect of catch rate on the financial performance of a representative Mediterranean artisanal fishing vessel*

other parameter values (i.e. price, utilization rate, etc.) remain at their baseline levels. Boat income switches from positive to negative if catch rates drop below 4.2kg per day fishing, a figure which should be compared with the actual catch rate of 7.13kg per day, at which level boat income is €2716 per year. This gives us an indication of how far catch rates can fall before becoming unprofitable, though it should be noted that this really represents an average for all boats in the group, whereas in fact there is substantial variation in the performance of individual operators around the mean. More importantly, however, the results draw attention to the fundamental dependence of the fishery on the state of the natural resource. Whatever may impact negatively on fish stocks – higher fishing mortality, pollution incidents, environmental perturbations – will translate into lower catch rates, and force the exit of some of the more financially marginal operators.

3.4 Attitude and opinion surveys

Public attitudes are increasingly influential in shaping public policy, particularly as it relates to the environment, and it is useful to be able to assess people's attitudes on specific issues and the factors that determine them. In marine aquaculture, for example, attitude surveys have highlighted a number of connections between the social acceptability of the industry and its environmental performance (Katranidis et al, 2003; Whitmarsh and Palmieri, 2009). Regional differences in attitudes towards aquaculture development are apparent, and this has considerable policy relevance since coastal districts where people are more favourably disposed towards fish farming may sensibly be chosen as the preferred candidates for site selection, other things being equal. Canvassing public opinion can also be useful in other areas of coastal zone management, a good illustration of which is the use of importance and satisfaction ratings to recreational activities in the Florida Keys, so as to enable resource managers to identify key areas of concern and prioritize them for action (Leeworthy and Wiley, 1996 and 1997).

In this section we will focus on consumer attitudes and their role in seafood product markets. One of the most interesting areas of study relates to purchase decisions (Hermann et al, 1994; Nauman et al, 1995; Al-Mazrooei et al, 2003; Trondsen et al, 2003), and the particular influence that attitudes play in determining fish consumption patterns. Technically this can be quite a complex area, and some studies of seafood product markets have involved the application of techniques such as conjoint analysis (Holland and Wessells, 1998) and choice experiments (Jaffry et al, 2004) that are beyond the scope of this book. The aim here is less ambitious, the purpose being to show how fairly simple methods can be applied to consumer survey data to test for attitude-behaviour relationships.

To illustrate what is involved, let us suppose that a small-scale exploratory study has been undertaken to see whether consumer attitudes towards the marine environment (expressed as concern about overfishing) have an influence on purchases of ecolabelled seafood. The research has been designed with the aim of collecting a limited amount of data in a short period of time, prior to conducting a larger and more comprehensive consumer survey of purchasing behaviour. The dataset consists of responses from 50 consumers, summarized in Table 3.4. The variables are all dichotomous, meaning that they are treated as binary categories taking one of two values (usually 0 or 1). These are defined and coded as follows:

ACTION: Ecolabelled seafood purchased weekly (Yes = 1, No = 0)
ATTITUDE: Serious concern about overfishing (Yes = 1, No = 0)
GENDER: Male = 1, Female = 0
AGE GROUP: Over 30 years of age (Yes = 1, No = 0)

Though we are interested primarily in the relationship between environmental attitude and purchase frequency, two attribute variables (GENDER and AGE GROUP) have been included, since it is believed that they may also be influential.

Table 3.4 *Illustrative data for a small-scale exploratory study of consumer attitudes*

Case	Action	Attitude	Gender	Age group
A1	1	1	1	0
A2	1	1	1	0
A3	1	0	0	0
A4	1	1	0	0
A5	1	1	0	0
A6	1	1	1	1
A7	1	1	1	0
A8	1	0	1	1
A9	1	0	0	0
A10	1	1	1	1
A11	1	1	0	1
A12	1	1	0	1
A13	1	0	0	1
A14	1	1	1	1
A15	1	0	0	1
A16	1	0	0	1

A17	1	1	1	0
A18	1	1	0	0
A19	1	1	0	1
A20	1	1	0	1
A21	1	1	1	0
A22	1	1	0	1
A23	1	1	0	1
A24	1	1	0	0
B1	0	1	1	0
B2	0	0	1	0
B3	0	0	1	0
B4	0	0	1	0
B5	0	0	1	0
B6	0	0	1	0
B7	0	0	1	0
B8	0	0	0	0
B9	0	0	1	0
B10	0	0	1	0
B11	0	0	1	0
B12	0	0	1	1
B13	0	1	0	0
B14	0	0	1	0
B15	0	0	1	0
B16	0	1	1	0
B17	0	0	1	0
B18	0	0	0	0
B19	0	0	0	0
B20	0	0	1	1
B21	0	0	1	0
B22	0	0	1	0
B23	0	0	1	0
B24	0	0	1	0
B25	0	0	1	0
B26	0	0	1	0

One of the ways in which we can summarize the data and also test the relationship between attitude and purchasing is by using a contingency table (Table 3.5), which cross-tabulates the number of observations in each category. The survey results show that 21 out of the 50 respondents expressed serious concern about overfishing, of which 18 (nearly 87 per cent) stated that they purchased ecolabelled seafood on a weekly basis. By contrast, 29 out of the 50 were not concerned with overfishing, of whom six (21 per cent) bought ecolabelled seafood. This pattern of results appears to suggest that the two variables are not independent of each other, but a more formal way in which this can be established is by using a chi-square test. This is based on a comparison between the observed and the expected distribution of responses across the four sub-categories (i.e. the pattern occurring on the basis of chance alone). SPSS

(Statistical Package for the Social Sciences) and most other statistical computer packages will include this function as routine, and will also test whether the result is statistically significant. In this case the calculated chi-square statistic is 20.3, which is significant at the 1 per cent level. What this means is that the two variables are very likely to be connected, and though the result cannot 'prove' causation, it is not unreasonable to infer that people's attitudes towards the marine environment are exerting an influence on their actions as seafood consumers. As an exercise, the reader is invited to use the data in Table 3.4 to test for the influence of the gender and age variables on the frequency of seafood purchases.

Table 3.5 *Contingency table showing the relationship between consumer attitudes and seafood purchasing behaviour*

		Concern about overfishing		
		NO	YES	TOTAL
Weekly purchase	NO	23	3	26
of ecolabelled	YES	6	18	24
seafood	TOTAL	29	21	50

3.5 Conclusions

Decision-makers and planners require information on the use of marine living resources, and the costs and benefits of alternative exploitation patterns. The main information needs for the fisheries sector relate to income and livelihoods, food security, trade performance and economic efficiency. Socio-economic research can provide this information, which may be based on existing data previously collected for other purposes (i.e. secondary), or original data collected specifically for the project in question (i.e. primary). There is reasonably good publicly available production data on global capture fisheries and aquaculture, and also per capita fish consumption for selected years, but very little information which would allow us to draw inferences about the economic value of this production and consumption, or the marine resources from which they are derived. Moreover, the geographical scale of fisheries and aquaculture data is typically at the level of countries or sea areas, which is obviously of no use at all if we are trying to answer the socio-economic questions of a fishing community at a specific port. For this reason it is often necessary to collect data from primary sources using survey-based methods involving questionnaires. We have focused on two types of survey: (i) cost and earnings studies, which are used to assess the financial and economic performance of commercial fisheries and (ii) attitudes and motivation surveys, the information from which may be of interest in its own right or (as in the consumer survey example) as a possible determinant of other variables such as purchasing behaviour.

Obtaining socio-economic information involves a cost, particularly where surveys are concerned, and this must be balanced against the value of the data collected. There are several aspects to this trade-off, shown most clearly between sample size (which affects the expense of the survey) and sampling error (which affects reliability and quality of results). It is worth emphasizing the point that larger sample sizes generate more accurate estimates. Additionally, large-scale data collection and analysis can be time-consuming, and a long delay in generating information may be unacceptable to policy-makers who need to make decisions with some urgency. The supreme example of this kind of problem is bioeconomic modelling, which at its most sophisticated can be highly data-intensive and extremely costly. Once again, the challenge is magnified when dealing with fisheries in developing countries where even the most basic data (landings, vessel numbers, etc.) may be lacking or of questionable credibility. Building up a picture of the socio-economic condition of the fisheries means, therefore, that one is starting from a very low base. In these circumstances there may be no choice but to use simpler and quicker methods of obtaining information, a fact that has been recognized in approaches to data collection such as Rapid Rural Appraisal (McCracken et al, 1988; Townsley, 1996).

4
Project Appraisal in Fisheries and Aquaculture

4.1 Introduction

Projects have been described as 'the cutting edge of development' (Gittinger, 1982), and since much of this book is concerned with the development of marine fisheries, it behoves us to consider some of the distinguishing features of fisheries and aquaculture projects. Fisheries development has had rather a disappointing track record, and this can be linked to the fact that quite a high proportion of projects have produced results which were below expectations. By their nature, all projects are subject to risk, but there are a number of special characteristics of capture fisheries that make them unique and which need to be taken into account if project failure is to be avoided. We have already come across two of these, one being the common pool nature of the natural resource and the other being the variability of catches. The significance of the first of these is that fisheries development projects that increase total catching capacity may, if no regard is paid to the finite productivity of the fish population, result in lower overall catches, or even stock collapse. The externalities of increased fishing intensity translates into lower catch rates for individual fishermen who share the common pool resource, an effect that will need to be anticipated in any prospective investment decision (e.g. purchasing a new vessel). The second important feature, catch variability, arises from environmental perturbations and fluctuations in fishing intensity. Variability implies risk, which for some fisheries can be very great and which needs to be factored into project appraisals. Aquaculture does not suffer from the common pool problem to the same degree as capture fisheries, but it nevertheless faces financial hazards deriving from production and market uncertainty (Kam and Leung, 2008). For this reason, risk analysis needs to be incorporated into any appraisal of aquaculture projects.

In the previous chapter we discussed sources of data in fisheries and aquaculture, and particular attention was given to cost and earnings studies and how they can be used as the basis for simple financial modelling. Here, we extend the discussion by showing how such data can be incorporated into investment decisions using the basic arithmetic of capital budgeting within a discounted cash flow (DCF) framework. We then develop the analysis by demonstrating how project viability may be impacted by adverse biological changes (falling catch rates) and the effects of parameter variability giving rise to risk. However, while it may be appropriate for private sector investments, data obtained from cost and earnings studies cannot by itself be used in the appraisal of projects that affect the welfare of the community at large. This is because the financial flows associated with a project may not equate with the wider social benefits and costs, a situation which for fisheries and aquaculture may arise because of externalities associated with environmental impacts. This subject is addressed in the latter part of the chapter.

4.2 The time dimension of investment in fisheries

Investment projects involve the use of valuable resources – human, manmade and natural – and the question that has to be confronted is whether such resources could be put to better use elsewhere. That is the purpose of project appraisal. A key feature of investment is that the costs incurred and the benefits generated arise over time, the profile being such that net benefits are typically negative in the early years, only later yielding a positive net return. The reasons for this are seen most clearly in the case of projects involving heavy initial capital expenditure (e.g. vessel purchase, harbour construction, artificial reef deployment, etc.), but we should also recognize that 'investment', in the context of renewable resources such as fish stocks, can also refer to the deliberate decision to defer their exploitation. The creation of a fisheries exclusion zone, for example, implies a loss of harvestable catch in the short run, in the hope of yielding a greater return at a future date and over an extended period. Indeed, many forms of fisheries management that have a conservation goal can be interpreted in this way, where the aim is to invest in the fish stock by reducing harvesting pressure and allowing potential yield to increase. In this sense, all policy interventions can be construed as projects, and it might reasonably be argued that they should be evaluated within a framework that properly accounts for benefits and costs. The performance of fisheries management might be somewhat different if this practice were routine.

The way we deal with the time dimension in project appraisal is therefore crucial. Benefits and costs need to be measured in appropriate monetary units, and the standard procedure for evaluating the stream of net benefits is to discount them according to when they are expected to occur. The logic behind discounting is that money has a time value, specifically that a given sum (e.g. €100 today) is worth more than the same sum in (say) ten years' time. This may be due to the fact that borrowed capital incurs interest, or because accumulated funds could alternatively earn interest if invested elsewhere. The normal practice in project appraisal is to convert all values to their present-day equivalents. The key question, therefore, is this: if a project is expected to earn €X at some future date, what is that €X worth in contemporary terms? We thus need to find the present value of future net benefits, and the sum we aim to calculate is termed net present value (NPV). NPV is the main criterion for deciding whether a project should go ahead, and the discounting procedure is used to calculate it through the formula:

$$\text{NPV} = \frac{(B_0 - C_0)}{(1 + r)^0} + \frac{(B_1 - C_1)}{(1 + r)^1} + \ldots\ldots + \frac{(B_n - C_n)}{(1 + r)^n}$$

where:

$B_0\ldots B_n$ = benefit expected in each year 0 to n
$C_0\ldots C_n$ = costs incurred in each year 0 to n
r = discount rate (representing the annual percentage cost of capital)

The reader should note that, in practice, the choice of discount rate will vary between whether we are considering a private sector investment or a social project. At this stage of the discussion, it might be simplest to think of r in terms of the former.

NPV is used as a decision criterion for deciding whether or not investment in a fisheries project should be accepted, the rule being: if NPV is greater than zero, the project is worth undertaking; otherwise, it is not. However, since a project will implicitly yield its own rate of return, this can also be compared with the interest rate, representing the opportunity cost of the capital invested in it. An alternative decision criterion that is often used alongside NPV is the internal rate of return (IRR), which is defined as the rate of discount which reduces the net present value of the income stream to zero. In this case the decision criterion is: If IRR is less than cost of capital (= the discount rate), then it pays to invest in the project; otherwise, it does not.

4.3 Financial appraisal of investment in fisheries

4.3.1 Project with constant catch rate

To illustrate the arithmetic of calculating NPV and IRR, consider an example of the proposed investment in a fishing vessel. The benefit and cost categories correspond to those of the artisanal fishery discussed in the previous chapter, but now include data on the expected capital outlay at the start of the project (year 0). The investment time horizon is ten years (i.e. years 0 to 9), over which period the annual net revenue stream is assumed to be constant (Table 4.1).

The revenue and costs are governed by the following parameter values:

Price = €10 per kg
Vessel utilization = 220 days per year
Catch rate = 8kg per day
Running costs = €7.5 per day
Fixed costs = €4500 per boat year
Crew share = 0.4 as a proportion of net revenue
Capital outlay = €30,000 per boat
Discount rate = 8%

In this example it is assumed that the resource potential is large enough to withstand the entry into the fishery of similar vessels. This implies that the exploited stocks will not be depleted, and catch rate remains unchanged.

Though the project is expected to generate constant positive cash flows from year 1 to year 9, the effect of discounting is to devalue these amounts according to how far into the future they accrue. For example, the anticipated cash flow of €5070 in year 9, when discounted at 8 per cent, is worth only €2536 in present value terms (since €2536 = €5070/(1.08^9)). The relationship between future and present values can be understood more clearly if we remember that discounting is the reverse of compounding. If we were to invest €2536 now at 8 per cent compound interest over nine years, it would grow to €5070 (since €5070 = €2536*(1.08^9)). The sum of the discounted cash flows from years 1 to 9 totals €31,672, and if we deduct from this the initial capital outlay of €30,000 we are left with €1672, which is the NPV. Since this is positive, the project is considered financially worthwhile and should go ahead.

The alternative project selection criterion is IRR, and this can best be explained diagrammatically. Figure 4.1 shows the relationship between NPV and the discount rate, and in the present example it is the upper line that is relevant. Higher discount rates imply an increasing cost of capital, which necessarily reduces the NPV. Graphically it can be seen that the line cuts the zero axis at a discount rate of just above 9 per cent, and this defines the project IRR. Since this is greater than the 8 per cent discount rate (which effectively measures the cost of financing the

Table 4.1 Cash flow for fisheries project assuming constant catch rate

Item	Year									
	0	1	2	3	4	5	6	7	8	9
Total revenue		17,600	17,600	17,600	17,600	17,600	17,600	17,600	17,600	17,600
Running costs		1650	1650	1650	1650	1650	1650	1650	1650	1650
Vessel fixed costs		4500	4500	4500	4500	4500	4500	4500	4500	4500
Crew payments		6380	6380	6380	6380	6380	6380	6380	6380	6380
Capital outlay	30,000									
Net revenue	0	15,950	15,950	15,950	15,950	15,950	15,950	15,950	15,950	15,950
Cash flow	−30,000	5070	5070	5070	5070	5070	5070	5070	5070	5070
Discounted cash flow	−30,000	4694	4347	4025	3727	3451	3195	2958	2739	2536
NPV =	1672									
IRR =	9.3%									

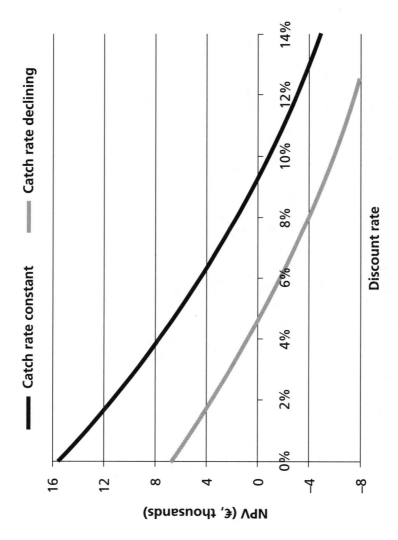

Figure 4.1 *NPV as a function of discount rate: comparison of two fisheries projects*

project), it again confirms our earlier verdict that investing in the fishery is worthwhile.

4.3.2 Project with falling catch rate due to stock depletion

Now let us consider the same project, but see what happens to financial performance if we suppose that not just one but several vessels enter the fishery, attracted by the lure of profit. If this is sufficient to deplete fish stocks, it will be reflected in the physical productivity of all participating vessels. To forecast the trend in catch rates, we would need to have a knowledge both of the planned expansion of total fishing effort and of the underlying yield-effort relationship (Cruz-Trinidad, 1990; Garrod and Whitmarsh, 1991). However, to demonstrate how even a modest decline in stock abundance may significantly affect the viability of the project, we will rework our example by assuming that catch rates fall by 2 per cent per annum across the life of the project.

The results presented in Table 4.2 reveal several consequences. As expected, total revenue declines, but so too do crew payments. This is to be expected, since crew are paid a share (40 per cent) of the net value of the catch and, as such, anything which reduces catch will impact adversely on labour earnings. Under this reward system the crew may be regarded as co-venturers with the vessel owners in the whole fishing enterprise. Falling total revenue necessarily means that cash flow also declines over the ten-year planning horizon, but crucially NPV now becomes negative (−€3970). What was previously a profitable investment is now unprofitable. Figure 4.1 shows NPV over the whole range of discount rates, the effect being to shift the NPV function downwards. The lower line on the graph now intersects the zero access at 4.5 per cent, which defines the IRR. If the cost of capital is 8 per cent, as we assumed previously, the fisheries project will turn out to be a poor investment. Failure to anticipate the effects of stock depletion and falling catch rates as a result of entry into the fishery will thus give an over-optimistic picture, by biasing profitability indicators upwards. We can think of this as another instance of the principle of market failure, in this case caused by the fact that the wrong signals are being sent out to investors and leading to overcapitalization (Cruz-Trinidad, 1990).

4.3.3 Project subject to risk

So far, we have assumed that the project cash flows are known with certainty, but in practice this is rarely the case. Uncertainty may arise either from internal sources (e.g. doubts regarding the technical capacity of a vessel) or from external sources (e.g. changes in the market price of fish, input costs, catch rates, quotas and other restrictions). Sensitivity analysis can be used in situations of pure uncertainty, where the aim is just to establish how sensitive a project is to a particular variable (e.g. a rise in

Table 4.2 *Cash flow for fisheries project assuming fall in catch rate of 2 per cent per annum*

Item		Year								
	0	1	2	3	4	5	6	7	8	9
Total revenue		17,248	16,903	16,565	16,234	15,909	15,591	15,279	14,973	14,674
Running costs		1650	1650	1650	1650	1650	1650	1650	1650	1650
Vessel fixed costs		4500	4500	4500	4500	4500	4500	4500	4500	4500
Crew payments		6239	6101	5966	5833	5704	5576	5452	5329	5210
Capital outlay	30,000									
Net revenue	0	15,598	15,253	14,915	14,584	14,259	13,941	13,629	13,323	13,024
Cash flow	−30,000	4859	4652	4449	4250	4055	3864	3677	3494	3314
Discounted cash flow	−30,000	4499	3988	3532	3124	2760	2435	2146	1888	1658
NPV =	−3970									
IRR =	4.5%									

fuel costs on profit), but by itself it tells us nothing about the likelihood of any of the risk-generating factors deviating from their baseline levels. However, where decision-makers have some knowledge of how such factors are likely to vary, it may be possible to quantify the probability distribution of profit outcomes using risk analysis. We illustrate how this may be done using our fisheries project.

Risk analysis is commonly performed using Monte Carlo simulation, which draws sets of values at random from each of the distributions of risk variables (e.g. price, variable costs, fixed costs, etc.), which combine to determine the outcome (e.g. profit, NPV, etc.). A number of iterations may be required if the true probability distribution of outcomes is to be estimated, and 500 might be considered the necessary minimum. Computers make this task straightforward, and while a number of specialist software packages are available (e.g. @RISK, Crystal Ball), it is also possible to undertake risk analysis using a spreadsheet program such as Excel (Seila and Banks, 1990; Judge, 1999; Smith, 2000). The basic requirement is obtaining information on the actual variation in each of the random factors, but in fisheries this may be difficult if data on the operating performance of the fleet have not been routinely collected. In the limiting case, the best and only approach may be to call upon the first-hand experience of fishermen and other experts regarding the likely highest and lowest expected values of performance-determining variables.

Given what is known in practice about commercial fisheries, we can reasonably conjecture that across the life of an investment project there will be year-to-year fluctuations in market conditions and catching opportunities. Let us suppose that a consultation exercise produces the following answers for the upper and lower boundaries for the main risk variables:

Price = maximum, €11: minimum, €9
Vessel utilization = maximum, 242 days per year; minimum, 198 days per year
Catch rate = maximum, 9.6kg per day; minimum, 6.4kg per day
Running costs = maximum, €8.25: minimum, €6.75 per day
Fixed costs = maximum, €4950: minimum, €4050 per boat year

For simplicity, we will assume that other factors (crew share, capital outlay and discount rate) are known with reasonable certainty and are thus treated as invariate.

In a situation where we have information only on the upper and lower boundaries of each of the risk variables, a symmetric triangular distribution can be a useful approximation (Engle and Neira, 2005; Kam and Leung, 2008). In Excel we can make use of the inbuilt RAND ()

function, which returns a random number between zero and below one. The syntax for the formula is:

$$= a + (b - a) * (RAND() + RAND()) / 2$$

where:

a = minimum value
b = maximum value

In Excel it is possible to perform a simulation either manually (by repeated pressing of the F9 key), or by automating the spreadsheet through the creation of a macro (Smith, 2000). The results presented in Figure 4.2 were generated manually and involved 500 iterations. The mean project NPV is €1587, indicating that the fisheries project is expected on average to be profitable, but it is clear by inspection that there is now a wide spread of possible NPV outcomes. In fact, given the chosen boundary values, there is now a 24 per cent chance that the project will return a negative NPV. This degree of risk may be unacceptable to a prospective investor.

4.4 Evaluating projects with external effects

4.4.1 Financial appraisal compared with economic appraisal

Where fisheries and aquaculture projects are being assessed from the standpoint of the community at large, it is necessary to adopt a different accounting convention from that based purely on financial performance indicators. Many types of publicly-funded projects are initiated with the purpose of generating benefits for diverse users, and financial objectives may be limited simply to cost recovery. Marine stock enhancement programmes, in which juvenile fish are released into the sea in the hope of recapture at a larger size, are an example of this type of initiative (Welcomme and Bartley, 1998; Bartley and Leber, 2004; Lorenzen, 2005). While the intention may be to raise catches and profits for a target group of fishermen, who may possibly be called upon to pay something for the privilege, the total beneficiaries are likely to include some who have not contributed to the cost of the programme. As such, the project will have produced unintended positive benefits that are not recouped financially by the funding body.

The reverse situation occurs where projects generate unintended negative effects, typically arising where there is damage to the marine environment that then indirectly imposes costs on others. Capture fisheries can create externalities in a number of ways, one example being the discarding of incidental fish, and another being sea-bed damage due to

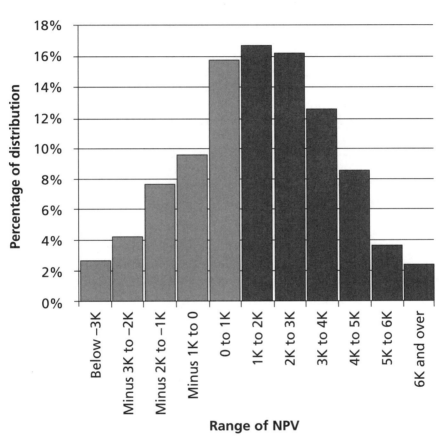

Figure 4.2 *Probability distribution of NPV for fisheries project*

trawling and other harmful gear (Pascoe, 1997; Holland, 2002). Aquaculture is also well known for producing a wide range of environmental impacts; some of which are positive, whilst others have been shown to give rise to significant external costs. Possibly the clearest demonstration of this is in shrimp farming, the growth of which in countries such as Thailand and Ecuador has been accompanied by effects that include destruction of coastal mangrove, loss of coastal protection functions, salinization of adjacent farmland and ecosystem effects on offshore capture fisheries. Externalities such as these need to be factored into the benefit and cost calculations if we are to accurately evaluate aquaculture projects from a social perspective, and unless this is done, we will get a falsely optimistic picture of their true worth.

To illustrate the point, consider the case of a shrimp farming project where the site preparation involves the conversion of an area of mangrove to growing ponds. Benefits are represented by the value of the shrimp output, while the main internal costs are those directly attributable to production (site preparation, labour, feed inputs, etc.). Mangrove removal, however, is likely to entail a loss of direct use benefits, such as forest products, as well as indirect benefits associated with offshore fishery linkages and flood defence (Sathirathai, 1998; Sathirathai and Barbier, 2001). We may realistically assume also that any pollution from the shrimp ponds, due to saline intrusion into freshwater supplies and the run-off of agricultural chemicals, will cause further external costs. Table 4.3 shows how the internal and external costs may be structured within a project appraisal framework, the data adapted from an example given in Whitmarsh and Palmieri (2008). A *financial* analysis of the project would consider only the internal costs, whereas an *economic* analysis would include these as well as the external costs. The NPV profiles are presented in Figure 4.3, from which it is clear that at discount rates above 10 per cent the financial return from the project is positive, whereas the economic return is negative. In other words, what might be regarded as a worthwhile enterprise from the relatively narrow standpoint of a commercial investor should be viewed quite differently by the community at large. It is precisely this disparity that Sathirathai and Barbier (2001) highlight in their analysis of shrimp farming in Thailand, where a profit-driven expansion of coastal aquaculture occurred rapidly despite the fact that the net benefits to society were at best marginal. The point, of course, was that commercial fish farms did not have to account for external costs in their investment decisions.

Table 4.3 *Accounting for external costs in a shrimp farming project*

Item	Year					
	0	1	2	3	4	5
Value of output		18,000	18,000	18,000	18,000	18,000
Internal costs	6000	15,000	15,000	15,000	15,000	15,000
Net financial benefits	−6000	3000	3000	3000	3000	3000
Lost mangrove benefits		1000	1000	1000	1000	1000
Pollution costs		400	400	400	400	400
Net economic benefits	−6000	1600	1600	1600	1600	1600

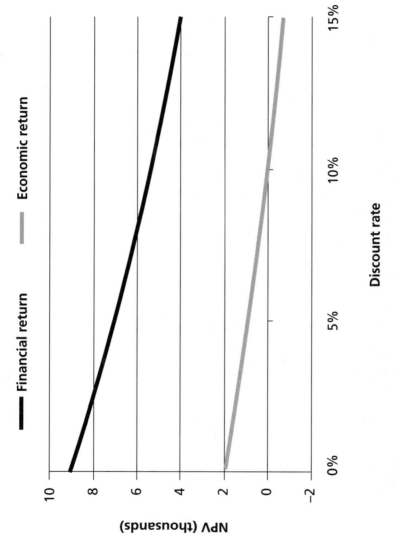

Figure 4.3 *NPV of aquaculture project comparing financial and economic return*

4.4.2 Problems of valuing external benefits and costs

To undertake this kind of exercise, however, presupposes that we can measure the external benefits and costs of a project in monetary terms. In practice the task is complicated, for two main reasons: indirect effects and absence of market prices.

(i) Indirect effects

Many of the wider effects of projects are indirect and hard to trace, as in the case of functional benefits provided by the resource (e.g. coral, mangrove, submerged aquatic vegetation) in supporting other economic activities. Ecological linkages are especially difficult to evaluate. The Mediterranean seagrass *Posidonia oceanica*, for example, is known to be an important food source and habitat for many types of marine organism (Holmer et al, 2003), and any reductions in seagrass cover caused by trawling or aquaculture will thus indirectly affect productive capacity and fishing potential in the ecosystem as a whole. While it may be possible to assess the damage to the resource from (say) sedimentation from fish farm cages, it is less easy to quantify the connection between that and the resulting output. One way in which this difficulty has been tackled by economists has been to estimate the relationship between fisheries production and critical wetland habitat, a statistical approach that relies on the availability of a reasonably long time series of data (Grigalunas and Congar, 1995). A key aim of such research is to separate out the contribution made to production by human input (e.g. fishing effort) from natural input (e.g. wetland area), and thus to answer the question by how much production would fall if habitat were reduced by a given amount. So long as a price can be attached to output, it is then possible to derive an implicit value for the habitat itself. Indirect effects of aquaculture projects may also be difficult to measure accurately where multiple sectors and economic functions are impacted. A vivid illustration of this is given by Huang (1990), who catalogues the many ways in which aquaculture growth in Taiwan has caused land subsidence, with consequent damage to property and infrastructure. Attaching a monetary figure to these multiple externalities is necessarily a data-intensive and methodologically complex exercise, and the approach used by Huang was to construct an econometric model in order to account for changes in property values. The results indicated that, on balance, the net social benefits of aquaculture were negative.

(ii) Absence of market prices

Projects which result in a commercially saleable product can be valued relatively easily using market prices, but in other cases this is not possible. Recreational fisheries are a good illustration of this, and where the resource is open access – as in the case of shore angling from public beaches – the user can be expected to enjoy the benefits free of charge. The 'product' of the fisheries is thus unpriced, and if we wish to value it in monetary terms we obviously have no market prices to use as a measuring rod. Environmental economists and others have developed a number of techniques for handling this type of problem (Barde and Pearce, 1991; Pearce and Moran, 1994; Hanley et al, 2001; Kalof and Satterfield, 2005), and here we can only give a very brief outline of this technically complex subject. The aim essentially is to elicit the preferences of target groups who may be affected by changes in the state of the environment, and specifically to derive their willingness to pay (WTP) for changes in the availability or quality of environmental goods and services. This may be based on observed market behaviour (e.g. calculating how much expenditure anglers actually incur in travel costs to visit a recreational site) or on hypothetical behaviour (e.g. asking how much people would be willing to pay to maintain a marine area exclusively for recreational use). The latter approach, involving what are termed stated preference methods, are increasingly applied to issues of environmental valuation, including those involving marine resources. The particular advantage of stated preference methods is that they can be applied to the measurement of not only the tangible use value of a marine resource (e.g. bathing, surfing, angling), but also its non-use value such as ecosystem services and biodiversity. One especially interesting application can be found in a paper by Glenn et al (2010), which evaluates the benefits and costs of protection for deep-water corals off the south-west of Ireland. It appears that the coral mounds offer very little use benefits, but potentially quite large non-use benefits by virtue of their conservation value. The corals are vulnerable to damage from trawling and certain other fishing methods, and a strong case can be made for limiting such harmful activity through area closures. However, marine protected areas (MPAs) entail a cost, both directly in terms of management and monitoring, and indirectly in the form of reduced fishing output. The issue thus hinges on whether the benefits of protecting the corals outweighs the costs, and the approach adopted by Glenn et al involved a questionnaire survey of residents in the Republic of Ireland in order to elicit their preferences for different MPA designations and management options. The survey showed that a majority of respondents were in principle willing to pay for the cold-water corals to be protected, with some three-quarters of respondents being prepared to pay more for fish taken from coral areas provided the management regime was 'environmentally responsible'.

4.5 Conclusions

Projects are the mechanism by which fisheries development takes place, and the appraisal of such projects at the inception stage is necessary to ensure that resources for development are used efficiently. Failed projects mean that development opportunities are lost. Standard decision criteria (e.g. NPV and IRR) can be applied for deciding whether projects should be accepted or rejected, but there are a number of unique characteristics of the fisheries and aquaculture sectors that should be incorporated into project appraisals. The tendency for vessel catch rates to decline due to the common pool nature of the resource needs to be factored into fisheries investment decisions, and unless this is done the financial indicators will be biased upwards. A further complication giving rise to uncertainty derives from catch variability, and this too needs to be accounted for in project appraisals. Sensitivity analysis is useful in answering 'what-if?' questions, but where data are available, risk analysis and simulation should be used in order to generate a probability distribution of all possible project outcomes.

Fisheries and aquaculture projects, whether undertaken by private sector organizations or public bodies, may often generate unintended side-effects (externalities) that affect the well-being of other groups of people. For this reason it is often appropriate to evaluate projects not just in purely financial terms, but from the wider perspective of the community at large. This is especially important where projects impact on the marine environment, since the evidence shows that this can give rise to major external costs and benefits. These may be positive, as in the case of (some) stock enhancement programmes, or negative, as in the example of mangrove shrimp farming. Putting a monetary value on externalities is in practice quite challenging, either because the effects are complex and hard to trace, or because there are no market prices for use as a benchmark. In recent years, progress has been made in developing methods to get round this problem, but there are many situations where monetary valuation of externalities is either not feasible or else not relevant because the project is being judged from a perspective other than that of economic efficiency. This has prompted the use of non-monetary scoring-based approaches, often conducted within the framework of multi-criteria analysis. This is a theme we deal with in a later chapter.

5
Markets and Prices for Seafood Products

5.1 Introduction

The material covered so far in this book has been concerned mainly with the factors affecting the production and supply of seafood products, and the demand side of the picture has largely been taken as given. Here we look at the role of markets in balancing supply and demand, a topic that we briefly encountered in Chapter 1 when discussing fluctuations in the price of internationally traded commodities such as fishmeal. Demand is an important determinant of the performance of the fisheries sector, though its effect is often more complex than policy-makers fully appreciate. Rising demand will stimulate the development of a fishery, but can also lead to over-exploitation if effort is not controlled. The use of measures such as ecolabelling and seafood certification is similarly ambiguous. Their purpose is to benefit fishermen by increasing consumer demand for products from 'sustainably managed' fisheries, but they run the risk that higher prices for the ecolabelled product will itself increase the incentive to intensify fishing and potentially undermine the management regime. Quota management is another policy area where the interaction between supply and demand needs to be considered, as evidenced by the fact that reductions in TACs and landings are likely to translate into higher market prices. For fishermen this may offer some degree of compensation for the enforced cutback in catches, but by the same token consumers will lose out. As well as in policy, a knowledge of markets and prices is also relevant in commercial decision-making within the fisheries and aquaculture sector. Project appraisal based on decision criteria such as NPV and IRR, which we examined in the previous chapter, requires a forecast of the stream of future profit, which in turn will depend on an assumption regarding market conditions over the time horizon of the planned investment. It obviously makes a difference to the viability of a project whether market prices are expected to rise or fall in real terms. Yet another area of decision-making where market information is essential is in new product development. A firm offering a differentiated or unique seafood product is confronted with the problem of not knowing how consumers are likely to respond, and would undoubtedly need to undertake some form of market research in order to make decisions about pricing strategy, advertising expenditure, target market, etc.

5.2 Markets and prices – some basic analysis

5.2.1 Shifts in supply and demand

In a free market, the price of a traded good or service will rise or fall as a result of changes in supply or demand. We need to be clear on the definition of these terms. *Demand* refers to the behaviour of buyers under a given set of market conditions, and specifically the quantity they wish to purchase at each and every price. *Supply* refers to the behaviour of sellers, and is similarly defined with respect to their willingness to offer goods for sale. A basic premise in economics is that price will have an inverse relationship with the quantity demanded (i.e. the higher the price, the lower the quantity purchased) and a direct relationship with the quantity supplied (i.e. the higher the price, the greater the quantity that sellers wish to offer for sale). There will be a unique price which brings the quantities demanded and supplied into balance, and changes in the underlying conditions of demand or supply will cause this equilibrium price to change. Factors affecting demand conditions include per capita income, the price and availability of other goods (substitutes or complements), product quality, consumer tastes and preferences, as well as other influences such as cultural norms relating to diet. On the supply side, factors include the production technology, the costs of inputs, resource abundance, enterprise risk, the profitability of alternative uses of capital and regulatory controls on production. It should be noted that the conditions of supply in the capture fisheries sector are dissimilar in many important respects from those in aquaculture, mainly due to the differences in resource ownership and control over production.

Figure 5.1 illustrates the market consequences of a shift in demand. The *supply curve* (S) intersects the initial *demand curve* (D1) at an equilibrium price of P1, at which level the quantity bought and sold will be Q1. If we now suppose that the demand curve shifts outwards to D2, price rises to P2 and quantity to Q2. Though the underlying supply conditions are unchanged, sellers have responded to the higher price by offering more for sale. In other words, there has been a movement along the supply curve to accommodate the shift in demand. Figure 5.2 shows the situation where the demand curve remains unchanged, but the

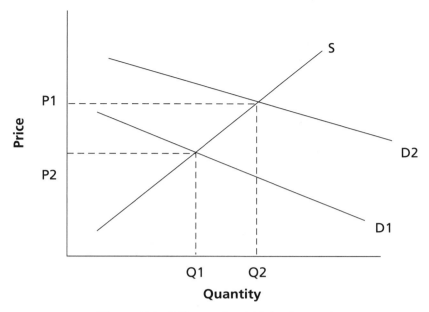

Figure 5.1 *Effects of a shift in demand*

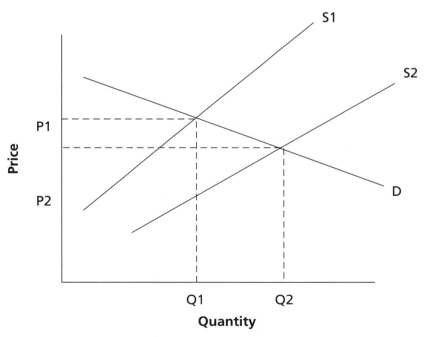

Figure 5.2 *Effects of a shift in supply*

supply curve shifts outwards from S1 to S2. In consequence, price now falls from P1 to P2, and quantity bought and sold expands from Q1 to Q2. What has happened in this case is that there has been a movement along the demand curve to accommodate the shift in supply. In both these examples, it is the combination of price and quantity adjustments that brings demand and supply into balance. There are a number of studies showing how seafood markets have been impacted by shifts in supply or demand, possibly the most famous of which is a paper by Bell (1968), entitled 'The Pope and Price of Fish'. In 1966 the Catholic Church relaxed its rules on the obligatory abstinence from eating meat at certain times of the year, a restriction which had hitherto helped to sustain consumption of fish on non-Lent Fridays. Using data for New England in the US, Bell showed that this caused a downward shift in the demand curve for fish. Theory predicts that this would cause prices to fall, and indeed the results showed that landing prices for fish fell by some 12.5 per cent on average during the nine months after the Papal Decree. This was anticipated to lead to a fall in industry revenue, with consequences for profits and jobs in maritime communities that were at the time already under pressure.

5.2.2 Elasticities of demand

It is useful to know in practice how responsive demand is to changes in different independent variables, and these can be summarized using the concept of *elasticity*. Three measures of demand elasticity are commonly identified:

- Price elasticity: the percentage change in the quantity demanded of a given product, divided by the percentage change in the product's own price.
- Cross-price elasticity: the percentage change in the quantity demanded of a given product, divided by the percentage change in the price of some other product (either a substitute or a complement).
- Income elasticity: the percentage change in the quantity demanded of a given product, divided by the percentage change in consumer income.

Where the response in the quantity demanded to changes in a given variable (e.g. own price, price of another good or consumer income) is more than proportionate, demand is referred to as being *elastic*. Where the response is less than proportionate, demand is described as being *inelastic*.

A very large number of empirical demand studies have been carried out over the years of seafood markets in various countries, and an overview of the topic is given in Asche et al (2007). A knowledge of

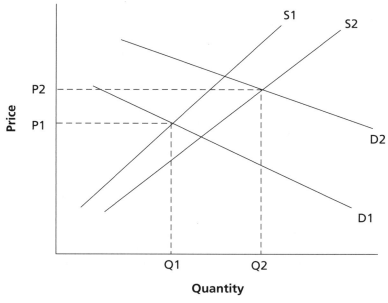

Figure 5.3 *Salmon price trend where demand grows more rapidly than supply*

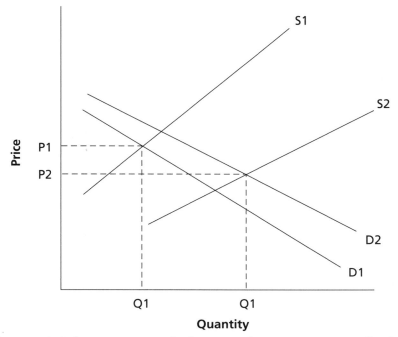

Figure 5.4 *Salmon price trend where supply grows more rapidly than demand*

demand elasticity can be important in understanding how the seafood sector will develop over time in response to changes in production, competition from alternative sources of supply such as imports or trends in consumer income. To take one example, farmed salmon production has increased greatly over the past three decades and there are questions over the ability of the market to absorb further supplies. In the UK, a study by Fousekis and Revell (2005) has found that the demand for salmon at the retail level is *price inelastic*, suggesting that a given increase in the quantity offered to the market will require a relatively large fall in price in order to bring supply and demand into balance. In this respect the situation appears to have changed from what it was in the late 1990s, when the prevailing view amongst UK salmon growers (if not amongst economists) was that there would be no significant price penalty consequent upon anticipated increases in production. From the producers' perspective, this looks to have been overly optimistic. The good news for the industry is that a number of studies indicate that the demand for salmon is *income elastic*, implying that if living standards and consumer incomes continue to rise the demand curve will shift outwards. The trend in price, however, will depend on whether the growth in demand occurs more rapidly than the growth in supply. Productivity in salmon aquaculture has risen rapidly in recent years (Asche et al, 2003), and if this continues it may exert a downward effect on price. In terms of our earlier analysis we can envisage two scenarios, illustrated in Figures 5.3 and 5.4. In the former case, the demand curve moves to a greater extent than that of supply and the price trend is upwards. In the latter, supply shifts more rapidly than demand and the price trend is downward.

5.3 Prices and landings

Capture fisheries offer an interesting example of the way price adjusts to changes in supply, and in so doing provide a graphic illustration of the 'law of demand'. In the short run, landings often have a dominant influence on the price of fish at first sale, and this relationship has been used as the basis of a very large number of studies that have attempted to identify so-called 'inverse' demand curves. Technically this is a complex area, but to give a flavour of what is involved we will use publicly available data on European fisheries to provide evidence that month-by-month fluctuations in landings are associated with corresponding price changes in the opposite direction.

A good example of such a relationship is the Spanish market for cephalopods (squid, cuttlefish and octopus), for which monthly data are available from the EUROSTAT database for the period January 1996 to December 2006. To start with we need to convert prices from nominal to real terms, which is done using a measure of inflation based on the

Harmonized Index of Consumer Prices (HICP). The difference between the original (nominal) and deflated (real) series is presented in Figure 5.5. Nominal prices show an upward trend, but this is partly explained by the underlying effects of inflation in the general economy. Once this is stripped out, the trend of real prices is much less obvious. If we now match these up with landings in the same month, we get the configuration of points shown in Figure 5.6. The pattern of observations strongly suggests that variations in landings 'trace out' the demand curve, and it is not a difficult task to estimate a line of best fit in order to derive what will obviously be in this case a downward-sloping relationship. The key result may be summarized in a parameter known as price flexibility, which is defined as the percentage change in price as a result of a 1 per cent change in landings (Jaffry et al, 1999).

For illustrative purposes it is legitimate to use a relatively simple procedure to obtain an order-of-magnitude estimate of price flexibility, though it needs to be emphasized that if we were undertaking this as a serious research exercise a more rigorous approach would be called for. To start with we would no doubt wish to include other explanatory variables, such as consumer income or the price of other species, in order to account for shifts in the demand curve throughout the ten-year period. In parallel with this, we would need to investigate the statistical properties of the time series themselves so as to avoid spurious results (Judge, 1999; Cameron, 2005). Adopting a 'quick and dirty' approach, however, our first step is to transform the original data into their natural logarithms and then to run a regression of real price (= dependent variable) on landings (= independent variable). The point of taking logarithms is that it measures the proportionate change in one variable as a result of a given proportionate change in the other, which is particularly useful for our purpose here. The regression coefficient in this case is −0.31, meaning that a 10 per cent increase in landings brings about a fall in price of just over 3 per cent, other things being equal. Strictly speaking, this figure refers to the contemporaneous impact of landings on price (i.e. within the same month), and the long-run effect may not necessarily be the same. Nonetheless, accepting for the moment that the result tells us something about market behaviour, the policy implications are quite important. Specifically, it means that regulatory controls (e.g. quota restrictions) that result in a *fall* in landings will be partially offset by a *rise* in market price. For fishermen this is some compensation for the fact that their catching opportunities have been curtailed, but the consumer who now has to pay the higher price will doubtless view the outcome rather differently.

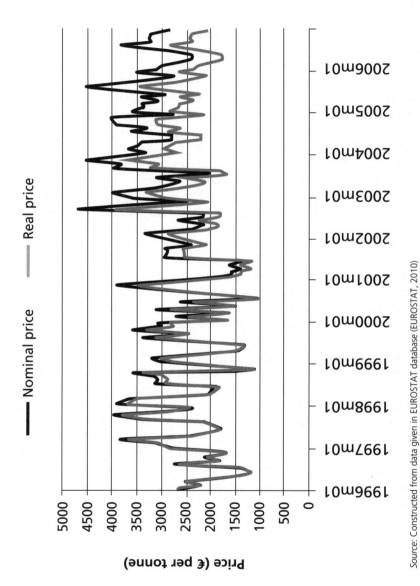

Source: Constructed from data given in EUROSTAT database (EUROSTAT, 2010)

Figure 5.5 *Spanish market for cephalopods: nominal and real prices*

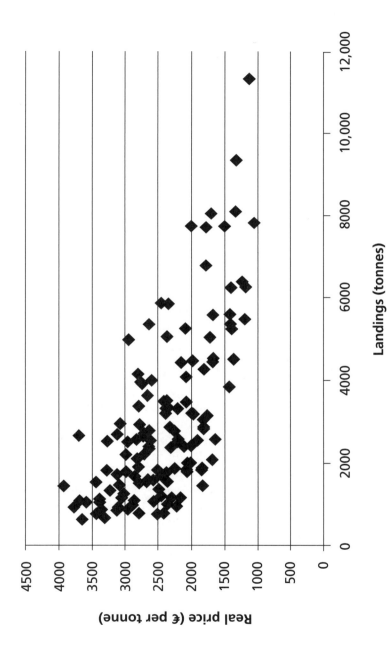

Source: Constructed from data given in EUROSTAT database (EUROSTAT, 2010)

Figure 5.6 *Spanish market for cephalopods: relationship between prices and landings*

5.4 Pricing, competition and market structure

Up till now we have assumed that prices of seafood products are set by the forces of supply and demand, mediated by the 'invisible hand' of competition. This state of affairs is one where individual sellers possess no market power, since they are compelled to take the market price as given and to respond accordingly as the business environment changes. In general terms, the factors that determine how much control a firm has over price derive from the structure of the market. The three main determinants of market power are:

- Uniqueness of the product (i.e. the extent to which one seller's offering is differentiated from that of others).
- Market concentration (i.e. the number and size distribution of firms within the market).
- Entry barriers (i.e. the advantage which established firms enjoy over potential entrants).

A market in which individual sellers have very limited market power would be characterized by having no product differentiation, a large number of competitors (i.e. low concentration) and few restrictions on entry. This description is probably a reasonably accurate characterization of the catching sector of the fishing industry in many countries, where fishermen in competition are landing similar species whose prices are determined at the quayside by the interaction of a large number of buyers and sellers. The innate characteristics of the product itself (particularly its perishability) also act as a constraining force on the price. Elsewhere, however, we encounter situations where firms may enjoy substantially more market power. In some countries the seafood processing sector is often dominated by only a handful of firms, each with a substantial share of the market and offering a distinctive range of differentiated brands. Having some discretion over price is in some respects a mixed blessing for firms, because it presents them with the problem of deciding the most appropriate price to charge. Unlike the fisherman who knows with reasonable confidence that his catch of (say) lobster is likely to fetch €22 per kilo, since that happens to be the current market price at the port of landing, a food manufacturer offering a branded seafood product enjoys no such certainty. In the former case, the seller does not need to make an explicit pricing decision; in the latter case, it does.

Generally speaking, the greater the novelty value of a product, the greater the marketing challenge, because almost by definition there will be no market information to use as a pricing benchmark. This kind of problem is typically encountered in aquaculture when the commercial production of new farmed species is being planned, since there may be considerable doubts about consumer acceptance and the price people may be willing to pay. Shang (1981) gives the example of the Pacific threadfin (*Polydactylus sexfilis*), a mullet-like fish which in the 1970s was being considered for commercial farming in Hawaii. At that time only small quantities were being landed from the local capture fishery, and household consumption of this species was correspondingly low. A consumer survey revealed that families might be prepared to buy farmed threadfin if supplies were stable and prices lower than those from the wild-caught fishery, and this information at least provided some basis for estimating the market potential of the proposed project. The problem of knowing what price to charge for a product is also illustrated by the recent trend towards product differentiation based on environmental attributes. Farmed fish marketed as 'organic' are expected to command a price premium, which should be sufficient to at least compensate growers for higher unit costs of production. Market research might ideally be undertaken in order to estimate the optimum price, though in practice most growers are likely to adopt a rule-of-thumb procedure of simply adding a mark-up on costs that is judged to be high enough to earn an adequate return on capital while being acceptable to consumers.

We have suggested that the structure of a market will dictate the pricing behaviour of firms, but it needs to be recognized that over time, market structure will evolve in response to competitive pressure. Industries made up of mature markets are often characterized by increasing concentration as less efficient firms exit or are taken over by more successful rivals, and this may be accompanied by the larger firms broadening the scope of their operations through diversification. In the seafood industry this tendency is exhibited more clearly in the onshore than in the catching sector, mainly due to the fact that economies of scale are of greater importance in the processing and distribution of fish than in its capture. In the UK, there has been a steady increase in the market share of large multiple food retailers, such that by 2006 almost three-quarters of all non-convenience grocery sales were accounted for by four companies, and over 30 per cent by just one (DEFRA, 2006). A high proportion of the sales of seafood products are dominated by these same retailers (Sea Fish Industry Authority, 2010). The current market structure should be seen in the context of a long-term historical decline in the number of small independent fishmongers in the UK, and wider structural changes within food retailing which encompass supermarket growth and changed food-shopping patterns.

It is interesting to compare the situation in seafood distribution with that at the production end of the supply chain, because although the pursuit of economies of scale has not tended to be a driving force in shaping the structure of the catching sector, it has certainly been influential in aquaculture. Tables 5.1 and 5.2 track the changes that have taken place in Scottish salmon farming between 2000 and 2008, a period that saw the industry face increasing competition from producers in other countries (notably Norway and Chile), and downward pressure on prices and profits. The number of operating companies fell from 90 to 35 over the eight years, and the number of sites from 346 to 257, but efficiency improvements due to technical innovation and scale economies resulted in an increase in average business size from 1433 to 3674 tonnes per company (Table 5.1). Evidence that smaller companies have been at a competitive disadvantage is shown by the comparative performance of those above and below the watershed size of 2000 tonnes per annum (Table 5.2). The market share of the larger companies, which are numerically in the minority, increased over the period such that by 2008 the top nine accounted for over 95 per cent of total production. If we now look at the labour productivity of firms in these two size categories, it is clear that those above 2000 tonnes p.a. have consistently outperformed those below this size threshold. This fact provides the likely explanation why market concentration has increased, since the productivity differential will have militated against the long-term survival of the smaller operators.

Table 5.1 *Salmon aquaculture in Scotland: resource use and business size*

Year	Companies (total number)	Sites (total number)	Production (total in tonnes)	Manpower (total number)	Business size (tonnes per company)
2000	90	346	128,959	1397	1433
2001	87	320	138,519	1257	1592
2002	84	328	144,589	1306	1721
2003	81	326	169,736	1217	2096
2004	69	315	158,099	1161	2291
2005	50	278	129,588	979	2592
2006	44	252	131,847	871	2997
2007	38	247	129,930	916	3419
2008	35	257	128,606	949	3674

Source: Fisheries Research Services (various years); Scottish Fish Farms Annual Production Survey

Table 5.2 *Salmon aquaculture in Scotland: market shares and productivity*

Year	Market share by company size				Productivity by company size	
	Production up to 2000 tonnes p.a.		Production above 2000 tonnes p.a.		Production up to 2000 tonnes p.a.	Production up to 2000 tonnes p.a.
	Number of companies	Per cent of market	Number of companies	Per cent of market	Tonnes per person	Tonnes per person
2000	75	25.8	15	74.2	59.7	114.0
2001	72	20.5	15	79.5	62.9	136.7
2002	69	23.8	15	76.2	74.4	130.6
2003	62	23.4	19	76.6	133.9	141.2
2004	51	16.7	18	83.3	102.5	145.7
2005	36	13.7	14	86.3	70.7	153.6
2006	33	9.3	11	90.7	59.9	179.5
2007	28	6.4	10	93.6	48.4	163.3
2008	26	4.9	9	95.1	42.9	152.6

Source: Fisheries Research Services (various years); Scottish Fish Farms Annual Production Survey

5.5 Consumer preferences and environmental scoring

The Papal Decree case study by Bell (1968), that we considered earlier, illustrates how consumer preferences may be altered by a specific institutional change, but the reality is that such preferences are constantly being moulded by the information that seafood buyers receive from a wide range of sources. Some of the information may have a positive effect on demand, which is obviously the intention in the case of brand-specific advertising by supermarkets, food processors and distributors, or generic promotional campaigns typically meant to make people aware of the health benefits of eating fish and fish products (e.g. omega-3 oils). In recent years, however, consumers have been treated to a much more complex set of messages, which in some instances have been quite deliberately intended to shift demand away from certain species of fish where there are concerns over sustainability. One method of doing this is via environmental scoring, whereby fish of a given origin are rated according to certain criteria that define the conditions under which they are caught or farmed. The scores may then be embodied in a 'traffic light' information system, the purpose being to enable consumers to identify fish which are produced sustainably ('to be eaten') and those which are not ('to be avoided'). In the UK, the main organization at the forefront of this approach in helping consumers make such intended informed choices is the Marine Conservation Society, while in the US a comparable role is taken by the Audubon Society, the Blue Ocean Institute and Monterey Bay Aquarium. Unilever plc, a large multinational with involvement in food handling and processing, has also adopted a 'traffic light' system as part of its internal purchasing protocol for ensuring that raw material supplies of seafood are obtained from sustainable sources.

It is not clear how far such initiatives have influenced the pattern of seafood demand, though the recommendations issued by the MCS in July 2010 are quite extensive, and list some 48 'Fish to Avoid' and 36 'Fish to Eat'. How receptive consumers are to this kind of exhortation remains to be seen, though there is little doubt that at the present time the seafood buying public are aware of some of the sustainability issues and certainly in the case of aquaculture products, and take account of environmental attributes in their purchasing decisions (Young et al, 1999; Muir, 2005). One indicator of this is that certain 'organic' labelled products command a price premium, and a study amongst Norwegian consumers has found that consumers were willing to pay some 15 per cent extra for organic and 'Freedom Food' salmon compared with conventional salmon (Olesen et al, 2010). In the UK context, it would seem that from a practical point of view one of the main problems with the MCS system is that the advice on choosing fish is often area, gear and date-specific, and that amount of detail may not always filter down to shop or restaurant level. As an example, one of the fish that consumers are recommended to avoid is plaice (*Pleuronectes platessa*) 'from the Western Channel, Celtic Sea, Southwest Ireland and West of Ireland Stocks' (www.fishonline.org). The MCS proposed alternative is to choose plaice from the North Sea or Irish Sea, which are classified as being fished sustainably, with the added recommendation that the choice should be in favour of fish from these areas that are caught using less damaging methods such as seine or gill nets. While this advice may be perfectly correct in scientific terms, anecdotal evidence suggests that, in the plaice example at least, such specific information is unlikely to be communicated to consumers. Where the system seems to work more effectively is when a product on the 'Fish to Eat' list has an ecolabel, notably those which have Marine Stewardship Council or Soil Association certification, or some other identifier (e.g. a tag to show that the fish has been caught using lines rather than trawls or fixed nets – though even here, line-caught fish are subject to some controversy as to whether this is a genuinely environmentally-friendlier method of fishing). However, until the fish labelling system in the UK is changed so as to require more detailed information on where and how fish are caught (and consumer understanding about fisheries is improved in order to interpret this), the general problem of communicating to consumers will remain.

5.6 Conclusions

Seafood markets affect the fortunes of stakeholder groups at all stages in the fisheries supply chain, from producers through to consumers. Those involved in the economic management of marine living resources need to have an understanding of the forces that drive these markets, and particularly the factors that determine the price of individual species and products. In this chapter we have introduced a number of concepts that are relevant here, specifically *elasticity of demand* and *price flexibility*. The latter is especially useful to fisheries managers, because it can be used to predict the impact of changes in landings (e.g. due to quota reductions) on quayside prices. We saw also that the price formation process is dependent on the market power of individual firms, which may be considerable where a dominant share of the market is accounted for by a limited number of sellers. There is some evidence that industrial concentration increases over time, particularly in mature markets where demand is static, which is what has happened in UK food distribution where currently three-quarters of non-convenience grocery sales are in the hands of just four large multiple retailers. A similar trend is observable at the European level.

But as well as the mechanics of supply and demand, it is important to have some appreciation of the attributes of the products themselves and how these relate to consumer preferences. Recent years have seen much greater prominence given to the environmental and other managed attributes of seafood, with a number of conservation organizations adopting 'traffic light' systems to help consumers make informed choices about which products to buy and which to avoid. These efforts, in parallel with seafood certification and ecolabelling, are part of the growing trend towards the use of demand-side approaches to fisheries management. Consumer awareness initiatives of this kind are still in their infancy, and it is not clear yet whether they have significantly modified the pattern of seafood demand, but in principle at least they represent a potentially valuable step towards tackling the overfishing problem. It is important nonetheless for more research to be undertaken to establish their effectiveness and to see how they could be improved. Clearly, marketing will play a crucial role in this endeavour.

6
Assessing Pollution Damages to Commercial Fisheries

6.1 Introduction

In a previous chapter we looked at ways in which fisheries and aquaculture may impose external costs on society as a result of environmental degradation. This may be associated with, for example, sea bed damage, caused by certain types of fishing gear or habitat destruction through the building of fish ponds. Here we consider the reverse situation where fishing and aquaculture enterprises are themselves the 'victims' of events that impact negatively on the marine environment, which in turn affect the fortunes of the business. The focus here is on damage arising from anthropogenic activities within the coastal area, specifically marine pollution, our main concern being to develop a framework for measuring the cost of such externalities to the fisheries sector. Monetary estimates of marine resource damage provide important information that can be used alongside environmental impact assessments, and are typically used as the basis for compensation claims against responsible parties such as oil companies. By the same token, liability for damages also serves a deterrent function by acting as a tax on potential polluters. Quantifying damages in monetary terms is not always straightforward, however. Economic costs caused by marine pollution include clean-up operations, losses of income (e.g. to fishermen, mariculturists, hoteliers, etc.) and degradation of non-market environmental assets (e.g. loss of wildlife, oiled beaches, destroyed mangroves, etc.). Environmental degradation is the hardest to quantify because it involves no directly observable commercial losses, and the methods that have been used in such assessments have in the past proved controversial – as exemplified by the use of the contingent valuation method (CVM) in the aftermath of the *Exxon Valdez* oil tanker disaster, which estimated the lost existence value of the natural resources at $2.8 billion (Carson et al, 2003). Though the total economic damage to the natural environment caused by marine pollution incidents may be substantial, the emphasis in this chapter is their significance for the fisheries sector and its dependent communities. We start by reviewing the main sources of marine pollution and recent trends in reported incidents.

6.2 Indicators of marine pollution

Oil pollution is a particular hazard for fisheries and aquaculture, and over the past 40 years there have been a number of high-profile incidents which have caused serious damage to the marine living resources and the fisheries they support. Major disasters involving tankers or barges have included the *Torrey Canyon* (Scilly Isles, UK, 1967), the *Amoco Cadiz* (Brittany, France, 1978), the *Exxon Valdez* (Alaska, USA, 1989), the *Erika* (Brittany, France, 1992), the *Aegean Sea* (La Coruna, Spain, 1992), the *Braer* (Shetland Islands, UK, 1993), the *Sea Empress* (Milford Haven, UK, 1996), the *North Cape* (Rhode Island, USA, 1996) and the *Prestige* (Galicia, Spain, 2002). Historically these have not been the largest incidents in terms of the quantity of oil discharged, but the location and siting (and more particularly, the disaster response) was such as to cause major disruption to marine harvesting and culture activities in the vicinity. In 2010 the world was introduced to a new type of oil spill hazard following an explosion on the *Deepwater Horizon* drilling rig in the Gulf of Mexico, a disaster which at the time of writing this book was still unfolding. Within a few weeks of the blowout in April of that year the slick had already affected fishing and tourism in the Gulf states of Alabama, Mississippi and Louisiana. Whether the total cost of the incident exceeds that of the *Exxon Valdez* oil spill, hitherto the most serious in US history, remains to be seen (Cohen, 2010).

These singular events need to be seen in a wider context. Data on the number and size of oil spills over 7 tonnes from tankers, carriers and barges over the period since 1970 are published by the International Tanker Owners Pollution Federation (ITOPF), and are shown in Figures 6.1 and 6.2. Since the mid-1970s, when the number of reported oil spills worldwide peaked at 117, the trend has been downward (Figure 6.1). The corresponding figures for the total quantity of oil discharged has exhibited much greater variability, and some of the larger spikes in the graph (Figure 6.2) can be attributed to identifiable incidents such as the *Atlantic Empress* (287,000 tonnes, 1979), the *Castillo de Bellver* (252,000 tonnes, 1983) and the *ABT Summer* (260,000 tonnes, 1991). Oil spills below the ITOPF threshold of 7 tonnes are reported by a few countries, which in the case of the UK suggests that there are typically several hundred incidents per annum involving discharge into the sea from vessels and offshore oil and gas installations (Advisory Committee

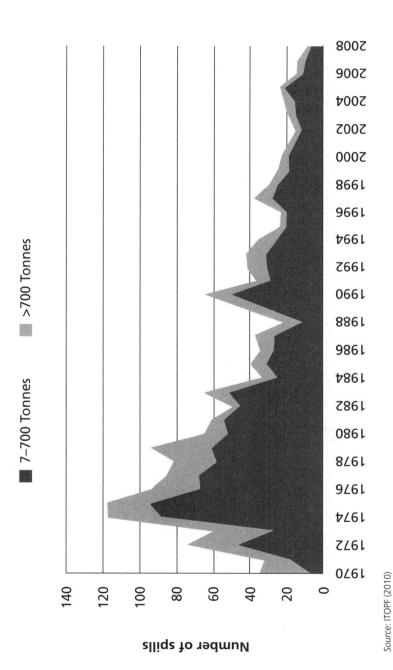

Source: ITOPF (2010)

Figure 6.1 *Oil spills from tankers, carriers and barges: number of spills according to size*

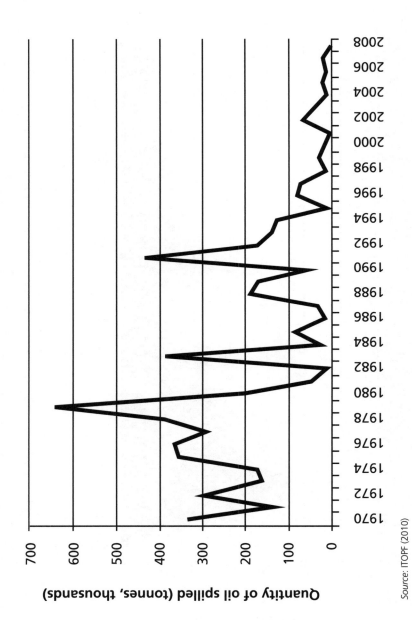

Figure 6.2 *Oil spills from tankers, carriers and barges: total quantities*

Source: ITOPF (2010)

on Protection of the Sea, 2008). In 2007 there were a total of 654 reported discharges, over 70 per cent of which were of mineral oil and nearly all the rest chemical (Table 6.1). Oil and gas installations located on the UK Continental Shelf (UKCS), and their associated supply vessels, are the originating source for almost three-quarters of all incidents. Most reported discharges are comparatively small (below 1000 litres), and in 2007 less than 1 per cent were larger than 50 tonnes (Table 6.2).

Table 6.1 *Marine pollution incidents around the UK in 2007: types of pollutant*

	Mineral oil	Chemical	Other	Total
England & Wales	116	0	1	117
Scotland	54	0	1	55
UKCS: oil & gas platforms	280	182	0	462
UKCS: vessels	20	0	0	20
Total	470	182	2	654

Notes: Numbers refer to reported discharges attributable to vessels and oil and gas installations within the UK pollution control zone. UKCS stands for UK Continental Shelf.
Source: ACOPS (2008)

Table 6.2 *Marine pollution incidents around the UK in 2007: volumes*

	Below 1000 litres	1–50 tonnes	Over 50 tonnes	N.K.	Total
England & Wales	65	3	1	48	117
Scotland	35	0	0	20	55
UKCS: oil & gas platforms	392	59	3	8	462
UKCS: vessels	9	3	0	8	20
Total	501	65	4	84	654

Notes: Numbers refer to reported discharges attributable to vessels and oil and gas installations within the UK pollution control zone. UKCS stands for UK Continental Shelf.
Source: ACOPS (2008)

Besides oil and chemicals, organic pollutants can also be damaging to fisheries. Marine contamination caused by sewage effluent may frequently lead to the closure of shellfish fisheries, principally due to health concerns. Additionally, however, the influx into the sea of land-based sources of organic material may trigger other effects, including nutrient enrichment and eutrophication. In extreme circumstances, these in turn may adversely affect fisheries by creating anoxic conditions that result in mass mortality. Organic pollution and eutrophication have also been implicated in the formation of harmful algal blooms (HABs), often described generically as 'red tides', which not only degrade marine ecosystems by adversely affecting other organisms, but also pose a serious risk to human health. Indeed, it is usually the health concerns that create the economic problem for fisheries, either as a result of precautionary action by management authorities to close an affected fishery, or simply through lost seafood sales. The processes involved in the formation of HABs are complex and not fully understood, but the costs they impose on fisheries are real enough and the frequency of their occurrence is increasing worldwide (Jin et al, 2008; Anderson, 2009). Variations in water quality as a result of organic pollution can be especially serious for aquaculture, and while there will typically be many external sources of pollution, it is clear that the operational characteristics of the fish farms themselves (e.g. high stocking densities) may exacerbate the problem. Low water quality may increase the vulnerability to disease, and seems likely to have been a contributory factor in the outbreak of ISA virus that hit Chilean salmon farming in 2007 and which has since devastated the industry.

6.3 Pollution damage to fisheries and other sectors

Marine pollution may impact on fisheries in a number of ways (Lipton and Strand, 1997), and these are summarized in Figure 6.3. In the first instance, the release of oil and toxic chemicals may adversely affect fishing opportunities through lower biological productivity due to outright mortality (fish kills) or impaired biomass growth (Bell, 1978), as well as possibly jeopardizing the long-term productive capacity of the industry as a result of habitat damage. This will reduce landings directly, as a result of lower catch per unit of effort, and also indirectly as fishing effort is withdrawn from the fishery. Secondly, consumer demand may fall due to concern about the edibility of the product and possible risks to health, and this will be passed through the marketing chain to the catching sector as merchants and processors cancel orders. Lower demand can in turn be expected to translate into reduced market prices. Thirdly, even in the absence of any biological injury, management authorities may restrict fishing and aquaculture in the areas affected by pollution, as well as prohibiting sales of fish (Whitmarsh and Palmieri, 2008). Such a response often accompanies oil spill incidents, and appears to be a routine reaction in the UK where there is the risk of contamination to shellfish beds caused by sewage effluent (Collins et al, 2003). Under all three scenarios, therefore, fishing and aquaculture firms can expect to suffer financially. Moreover, where vessels transfer out of the pollution zone in search of better grounds elsewhere, this is likely to impose an external cost on other fishermen already established in such areas, through greater competition for the shared resource.

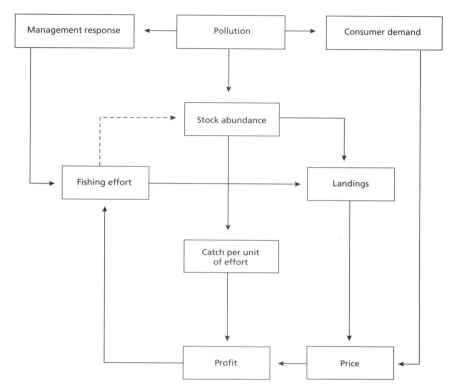

Figure 6.3 *Mechanisms by which pollution may impact on a fishery*

However, there will be wider consequences. Pollution events that cause landings and employment to be reduced will have repercussions for the regional economy and its dependent communities through what are termed *multiplier* effects, which define the total economic activity supported directly and indirectly by one industry or sector. To illustrate, consider the example of Scotland, where fisheries and aquaculture are important industries in the remoter rural areas where job opportunities are limited. Data published by the Scottish government gives an estimate of the employment multiplier for sea fishing as 1.64, meaning that for every ten jobs created directly in the catching sector, over six additional jobs are created elsewhere in the Scottish economy within supply industries (shipbuilding, transport, oil, etc.) connected with fishing. The employment multiplier figure for fish farming is 1.72, implying that every ten jobs in this industry support at least an extra seven amongst the industry's suppliers. The figures almost certainly underestimate the full economic impact of sea fishing and fish farming, and if we allow for induced effects – specifically, jobs created as a result of higher expenditure within households that are indirectly supported by these industries – we obtain employment multiplier estimates of 1.76 for sea fishing and 1.99 for fish farming (Scottish Government, 2010). The crucial point, however, is that multiplier effects operate in both directions – the expansion of an industry creates additional jobs in other sectors, but contraction will likewise cause such jobs to be destroyed. This means that an exogenous shock such as a pollution event may adversely affect production and employment, not just in capture fisheries and aquaculture, but in the wider economy. An illustration of this is the response to the *Braer* oil spill, which occurred off the Shetland Islands (Northern Scotland) in 1993. This had serious consequences for local salmon farms as a result of the ban on sales, but the multiplier effects of this meant that the total economic impact on the regional economy would have been greater still.

6.4 Assessing the economic effects of pollution

6.4.1 Damage assessment methods

Bioeconomic models may be used to explore the effects of pollution on a fishery, and this approach has provided some useful insights into the factors affecting magnitude of economic damages. Collins et al (1998) developed a model of an open-access fishery and considered the effects of two types of pollution event, one chronic and the other acute. Effort is assumed to adjust to changes in biological productivity, but the model demonstrates that it is the speed of this response that determines the scale of economic damages caused by pollution. Specifically, it is shown that the more willing fishermen are to exit the fishery in the face of reduced profits, the lower will be the social cost, provided that the labour and capital can be productively used somewhere else (e.g. in another fishery). The spatial implications of pollution are considered by Collins et al (2003), using a model of a fishery in which there are biological and technical linkages between five adjacent ports. An acute pollution event in one area is assumed to result in the closure of a fishery, with two scenarios compared: in one, boats are free to move out of the affected area to seek fishing opportunities elsewhere; in the other, there is a ban on relocating. The basic conclusion is that economic damages caused by pollution depend on the way management authorities react to such incidents, a key result being that permitting vessels to relocate may attenuate the financial burden in the area immediately impacted by pollution, but at the expense of fishing firms in adjacent areas. Bioeconomic modelling is also used by Knowler et al (2001, 2002) to investigate the effects of nutrient loading in a fishery system characterized by complex ecological dynamics. The model is applied to the anchovy fishery in the Black Sea, an area where substantial nutrient enrichment had taken place throughout the 1970s but whose effect has been ambiguous. On the one hand, it has enhanced food supply and raised anchovy recruitment; on the other, it may have been a causal factor in the invasion of the exotic comb jelly *Mnemiopsis leidyi*, which is a predator of the anchovy. On balance, a policy of nutrient reduction would have had a positive effect on revenue and employment, so long as it succeeded in forestalling the ecological 'regime shift' that accompanied the invasion of *M. leidyi*.

In practice, damage assessment may need to be undertaken rapidly and with only limited data, and this often rules out the use of bioeconomic models. In the case of oil spills, monetary estimates may be based on: (i) compensation for damages claimed by fishermen and growers, as well as the amounts finally awarded; and (ii) assessment of damages derived from data collected for the purpose (e.g. a financial survey of individual producers), or indirectly using time series data on production and value for the fishery as a whole (Thebaud et al, 2004; Suris-Regueiro et al, 2007). Indirect methods of damage assessment are appropriate in circumstances where pollution incidents are large enough to have a measurable effect on total weight of fish produced and the market price, and have been used to estimate the economic losses to fishermen in a number of prominent tanker disasters such as the *Amoco Cadiz* (US Department of Commerce, 1983; Grigalunas et al, 1986), the *Exxon Valdez* (Cohen, 1995) and the *Prestige* (Suris-Regueiro et al, 2007). The same approach can be applied to other sources of pollution damage, one example of which is the study by Jin et al (2008) on the economic impact of the harmful algal bloom *Alexandrium fundyense* on the shellfish fisheries of New England (USA) in 2005. Because indirect methods using time series analysis have been extensively applied in practice, it is appropriate to examine them more closely before considering how they may be applied to data on an actual pollution incident.

6.4.2 Assessment using time series data

Estimating the losses to fisheries and aquaculture, caused by environmental perturbations such as pollution incidents, involves a comparison between the actual value of production after the incident with the value that would have been expected had the incident not occurred. Expected quantities and prices can be approximated by reference to data covering the period immediately prior to the incident, and if data are available after the event it may also be possible to use time series methods to estimate other influences such as trend and seasonality.

The theory underlying this method is depicted in Figures 6.4 and 6.5. Two scenarios are envisaged: one in which pollution impacts only on supply (e.g. due to closure of the fishery); and the other in which demand is also affected (e.g. due to consumer concerns about product quality). In the first case, the short-run supply function shifts to the left, causing market price to rise and making consumers worse off. If the rise in price

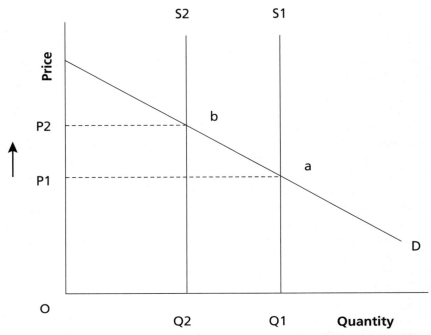

Figure 6.4 *Short-run effects of pollution in a fishery: shifts in supply*

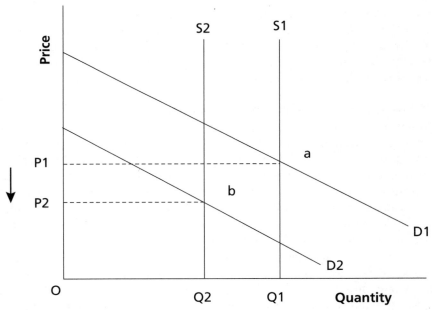

Figure 6.5 *Short-run effects of pollution in a fishery: shifts in both supply and demand*

is proportionately smaller than the fall in quantity harvested, sales revenue earned by producers will decline; if proportionately greater, revenue will increase. On the first diagram (Figure 6.4), the revenue change following the spill can be represented as the difference between the area of the rectangle P1-a-Q1-O and P2-b-Q2-O. In this example, sales revenue is shown as falling, but this result comes about because we have assumed that demand is relatively responsive to price (i.e. elastic). In other circumstances the result may be different, and in fact it is perfectly possible for producers to gain financially from a pollution incident if market scarcity drives the price up by more than the quantity has fallen. In the second scenario (Figure 6.5), the reduction in both supply and demand causes sales revenue to fall as a consequence of the combined effect of lower harvest and price. This can again be represented by the difference in the area of the rectangles P1-a-Q1-O and P2-b-Q2-O. The case described in Figure 6.5 is rather more difficult to evaluate empirically than the one in Figure 6.4, since it requires a forecast of what would have happened in the absence of the pollution event of both harvest volume and the price. It is nevertheless useful to be able to do this if we are interested in seeing how much of the economic cost of pollution is attributable to changes in production and how much to changes in price. One particularly good example of this type of analysis is in the case of the *Exxon Valdez* oil tanker disaster, where Cohen (1995) demonstrates that the drop in revenue to Alaskan salmon fishermen following the spill in 1989 was attributable to both lower harvested volume and lower price.

6.4.3 The Sea Empress case

The empirical problems of using time series data for damage assessment are illustrated by the case of the *Sea Empress* oil spill, which occurred in February 1996. The discharge of some 72,000 tonnes of crude caused a slick which affected much of the coastline of South Wales, an area of high environmental sensitivity, and which is valuable as a tourist location and for fisheries. Clean-up and salvage following the spill represented the largest category of economic cost (Moore et al, 1998), and it is testimony to the speed and efficiency with which these remedial actions were undertaken that the damage to the natural resources of the area was not greater. A voluntary ban on fishing was adopted, later made compulsory by a fisheries exclusion order which covered an area of over 2000km². The prohibitions were removed in stages over the subsequent months, commencing in May for finfish, but remaining in place until late August and early September for molluscan and crustacean shellfish.

The main difficulty in this case is that only annual data are available on the fisheries impacted by the *Sea Empress* spill, and just for the years since 1993. In Table 6.3 we show the weight and price of fish landed since this date, based on landings within the district covered by the South Wales Sea Fisheries Committee (SWSFC) District. The series are extended up to 1999, thus giving a picture of what happened three years before and after the incident. The statistical challenge is to separate the 'noise' from the 'signal', because it is clear by inspection that both the quantities landed and the prices vary substantially from year to year, and except for crustaceans it is by no means obvious that any abnormal event occurred in 1996. Landings of molluscs fell by a modest 11 per cent on the previous year, while for finfish they actually rose by 7 per cent. This increase may be due to the fact that a significant proportion of catches of demersal species originated outside the SWSFC District by vessels landing at the port of Milford Haven, but sourcing their catches from offshore fishing grounds in the Celtic Sea (ICES VIIg). As such they would not have been affected by the exclusion order, which covered only the inshore areas.

Table 6.3 *Landings of fish in South Wales before and after the 1996 Sea Empress oil spill*

Year	Finfish		Molluscs		Crustaceans	
	Quantity (tonnes)	Price (£ per tonne)	Quantity (tonnes)	Price (£ per tonne)	Quantity (tonnes)	Price (£ per tonne)
1993	2087	1536	8023	186	713	2242
1994	1966	1534	4149	205	711	1806
1995	1771	1344	6841	251	844	1751
1996	1898	1485	6116	356	343	1679
1997	2945	1747	8506	277	1016	1729
1998	2310	1476	5972	417	962	1737
1999	3476	1787	6714	241	853	1623

Source: South Wales Sea Fisheries District Committee (2010)

A more fundamental empirical problem is that this whole methodology of damage assessment is based on a comparison between actual and expected values, and the latter cannot be observed. The simplest practical approach is to compare landings and prices in the year of the oil spill with the corresponding figures for the previous year, but this is not really appropriate if fishing effort is on a rising or falling trend. That indeed was the case at the time of the *Sea Empress* incident in at least one sector, since we know that the fishery for whelk (*Buccinum undatum*) had attracted a substantial amount of investment in 1995 and was set to expand rapidly (Tingley et al, 1998). The expectation, therefore, was that landings of whelk in 1996 would undoubtedly have been higher than the year before had the exclusion order not been imposed, and hence a naive comparison between actual landings in 1996 and 1995 would certainly have underestimated the true cost of the fishery closure. In the case of the crustacean (mostly crab and lobster) fisheries, which was the sector most heavily impacted by the oil spill, there is no obvious disequilibrium, and the landings for 1995 can probably be taken as a baseline figure with which to compare the situation the following year. In the event, the value of crustacean landings fell by just over £900,000 between 1995 and 1996 (Figure 6.6), which on the face of it might be taken as a ballpark estimate of the loss to fishermen caused by the incident. The complication, however, is that landings in 1997 recovered sharply, exceeding the 1995 level (i.e. before the spill) by almost £280,000. It seems unlikely that this was merely fortuitous, but rather a consequence of the fishery closure in 1996 and the resulting increase in stock abundance. In other words, the value of landings in 1997 could arguably be said to be *higher* than expected had the incident not occurred, thus mitigating the damages.

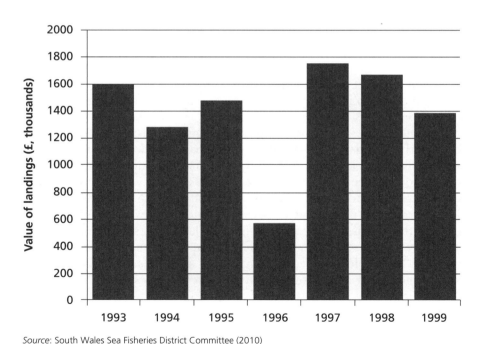

Source: South Wales Sea Fisheries District Committee (2010)

Figure 6.6 *Impact of the Sea Empress oil spill on the value of crustacean landings in South Wales*

6.4.4 The Prestige case

This incident occurred in November 2002, when the tanker *Prestige* ran into difficulties off the NW coast of Spain and sank with its cargo of 77,000 tonnes of crude oil. The subsequent spill caused serious ecological degradation, as well as adversely affecting the livelihoods of communities, particularly in the region of Galicia, who depended heavily on fishing and tourism (Garza-Gil et al, 2006a and 2006b; Suris-Regueiro et al, 2007; García Negro et al, 2009). A ban was immediately imposed on coastal fisheries, its coverage being most extensive during the first six months but remaining in force for some areas for several months longer. The size of the affected area meant that the clean-up operations and palliative measures were not finally completed until December 2004, expenditure on which was estimated to be some €509 million out of a total cost of €770 million (Loureiro et al, 2006). In fact, the latter figure almost certainly underestimates the full economic damage, since it takes no account of lost passive use values associated with the natural heritage of the Galician region. A recent study puts this damage alone at approximately €1.37 billion, an estimate based on household willingness to pay to avoid such a catastrophe (Garza et al, 2009).

The cost of the *Prestige* incident to the commercial fisheries of Galicia can be inferred from changes in landings, and here we are fortunate in having monthly data available through the Pesca de Galicia database covering the period when the spill took place. Though figures on both quantity landed and price only start from January 2001, this is sufficient to make a basic comparison between the state of the fisheries in the months following the oil spill with the corresponding period 12 months earlier. A summary of the changes is given in Table 6.4, where prices and values are expressed in real terms so as to remove the effect of underlying inflation. The impact of the fisheries closure following the spill shows up clearly in the sharp fall in the weight of fish landed throughout the period November 2002 to February 2003, with declines of lesser magnitudes in the months that followed up until the summer. By contrast, the movement of prices for the first seven months was in exactly the opposite direction to those of landings, suggesting that the scarcity effect of reduced supplies had impacted on the market. Elevated prices in the period immediately after the spill thus partially compensated fishermen for the drop in landings, a result reflected in the fact that the fall in money value was less than the fall in physical quantity. The change in the value of landings was nonetheless considerable – down €36.65 million (30 per cent) for the four months November to February compared with the previous year, and €8.22 million (7.5 per cent) for the period March to June.

Table 6.4 *Effect of the Prestige oil spill on fisheries in Galicia, NW Spain*

Date	Main variables during spill period			Change on previous 12 months		
	Landings (tonnes)	Real price (€ per tonne)	Value (€m)	Landings per cent	Real price per cent	Value per cent
2002: Nov	8995	3059	27.527	−27.2	+17.6	−14.3
2002: Dec	5699	3705	21.116	−47.0	+4.9	−44.4
2003: Jan	4894	3433	16.803	−46.1	+20.3	−35.2
2003: Feb	7397	2552	18.879	−25.9	+2.2	−24.3
2003: Mar	9739	2475	24.107	−15.0	+11.8	−5.0
2003: Apr	11,038	2232	24.639	−19.1	+6.6	−13.8
2003: May	9837	2739	26.944	−15.5	+14.4	−3.2
2003: June	10,201	2474	25.234	−5.9	−1.9	−7.7
2003: July	13,076	2411	31.530	+7.3	−12.5	−6.1
2003: Aug	11,206	2535	28.407	+0.2	−13.3	−13.1
2003: Sept	14,083	2368	33.343	+21.3	−3.4	+17.2
2003: Oct	13,250	2521	33.406	+13.0	−2.9	+9.7

Source: Based on data from the Pesca de Galicia database. Prices have been deflated by the Harmonized Index of Consumer Prices (HICP) given in EUROSTAT, taking January 2003 as the base month. Values are likewise in real terms.

With the benefit of several years' hindsight, and data to match, it is possible to make a more accurate assessment of the impact of the *Prestige* spill by separating out the influence of trend and seasonality on the pattern of Galician landings. The method adopted here is similar to that used by Jin et al (2008), and involves the construction of a regression model using monthly observations on the weight and value of landings for the period January 2001 through to December 2009. Variables included in the model are defined in Table 6.5, and the results presented in Table 6.6. Seasonality is accounted for by the use of 11 monthly dummy variables (January to November, with December being the reference category), while the inclusion of a trend variable allows for the influence of other factors either on the supply or the demand side that may have caused landings to change over time. Given what we know of the aftermath of the event, particularly the staggered reopening of fisheries in the affected area, the impact of the spill is assessed by three separate dummy variables covering the period November 2002 to February 2003 (SPILL1), March 2003 to June 2003 (SPILL2) and July 2003 to October 2003 (SPILL3). Results are shown for quantity and value, both measured in their logarithmic form so that the regression results can be interpreted as proportionate rather than absolute changes.

Table 6.5 *Variables used in the multiple regression analysis of the impact of the Prestige oil spill*

Name	Type	Definition and measurement
LNVALUE	DEPENDENT	Natural logarithm of the value of landings
LNQUANTITY	DEPENDENT	Natural logarithm of the weight of landings
M1	INDEPENDENT	1 for observations in January, 0 otherwise
M2	INDEPENDENT	1 for observations in January, 0 otherwise
M3	INDEPENDENT	1 for observations in February, 0 otherwise
M4	INDEPENDENT	1 for observations in March, 0 otherwise
M5	INDEPENDENT	1 for observations in April, 0 otherwise
M6	INDEPENDENT	1 for observations in June, 0 otherwise
M7	INDEPENDENT	1 for observations in July, 0 otherwise
M8	INDEPENDENT	1 for observations in August, 0 otherwise
M9	INDEPENDENT	1 for observations in September, 0 otherwise
M10	INDEPENDENT	1 for observations in October, 0 otherwise
M11	INDEPENDENT	1 for observations in November, 0 otherwise
TIME	INDEPENDENT	1 for observations in January 2001, increasing over time in monthly units to December 2009
SPILL1	INDEPENDENT	1 for observations in November 2002 through to February 2003, 0 otherwise
SPILL2	INDEPENDENT	1 for observations in March 2003 through to June 2003, 0 otherwise
SPILL3	INDEPENDENT	1 for observations in July 2003 through to October 2003, 0 otherwise

Table 6.6 reveals that the closure of the fisheries in the first four months following the spill had a statistically significant impact on landings, which can be measured by taking the exponential of the regression coefficient for the variable SPILL1 (–0.441) to give us a figure of 0.643. In other words, quantity landed throughout November 2002 to February 2003 was reduced to 64.3 per cent of what it would have been in the absence of the spill. During the next four months the impact is shown to have attenuated, since the regression coefficient on SPILL2 is now only –0.229, meaning that landings were lowered to 79.5 per cent of what would otherwise have been expected. In the final four months, though the regression coefficient on SPILL3 is negative, the result is not statistically significant. If we now repeat the exercise for value, the results imply that the closure of the fisheries in the first four months resulted in the value of landings being reduced to 66.2 per cent of their expected level, while in the subsequent period the reduction was more modest at 87.2 per cent. The regression coefficient in the final four months is again not

Table 6.6 *Results of the regression analysis of the Prestige incident*

Independent variables	Dependent variable			
	LN quantity		LN value	
	Regression coefficient	t-value	Regression coefficient	t-value
Constant	9.056	160.286	17.464	445.114
M1	–0.051	–0.761	–0.320	–6.843
M2	0.261	3.876	–0.326	–6.974
M3	0.406	5.940	–0.240	–5.056
M4	0.290	4.252	–0.305	–6.433
M5	0.285	4.175	–0.288	–6.077
M6	0.264	3.867	–0.323	–6.810
M7	0.384	5.625	–0.160	–3.376
M8	0.362	5.316	–0.132	–2.787
M9	0.365	5.349	–0.228	–4.823
M10	0.264	3.876	–0.217	–4.591
M11	0.175	2.605	–0.193	–4.139
TIME	0.003	6.874	0.000	0.534
SPILL1	–0.441	–5.724	–0.412	–7.690
SPILL2	–0.229	–2.993	–0.137	–2.578
SPILL3	–0.042	–0.546	–0.016	–0.301
N =	108		108	
R2 =	0.727		0.651	
DW =	1.892		1.850	
F =	16.308		11.446	

statistically significant. Overall, the results confirm that the greatest economic damage was caused during the immediate aftermath of the incident, with the value of landings being reduced by over one-third, but the effects were nevertheless still apparent, albeit in weaker form, up to eight months later.

6.5 Conclusion

External events such as oil spills and harmful algal blooms (HABs) may impact on fisheries in several ways, and their economic cost often needs to be assessed as a basis for compensation. This chapter has addressed the topic of marine resource damage assessment, which aims to establish the loss to society arising from degradation of the marine environment caused by pollution and other harmful events. Economic costs caused by incidents such as oil spills typically include clean-up costs, losses of income (e.g. to fishermen, mariculturists, hoteliers, etc.) and cost of degradation of non-market environmental assets (e.g. loss of wildlife, oiled beaches, destroyed mangroves, etc.). The financial burden on commercial fisheries may come about through biological injury to the natural resource, as may occur when toxic chemicals cause outright fish-kills, but may also arise through adverse market movements (e.g. because of concerns over food safety or action by management authorities to close a fishery affected by contamination). The total economic impact of pollution events typically extend beyond the fisheries sector, causing output reductions and job losses elsewhere in the regional community as a consequence of downward multiplier effects.

Pollution damage to marine resources and fisheries caused by oil spills have been studied *ex post* in a number of high-profile cases, and several methods are available for quantifying damages in monetary terms. Some categories of economic cost are relatively easy to assess (e.g. clean-up), others more difficult (e.g. destroyed habitat). This chapter has focused on economic costs to fisheries arising from lost production, the assessment of which in practice often involves the use of indirect methods that employ time series data on the quantity and money value of catches. Two oil-spill tanker disasters, the *Sea Empress* and the *Prestige*, were used to illustrate this approach. The main requirement is for an adequately long historical data series from which to form a judgement of what the expected landings from a fishery would have been in the absence of a pollution incident. In the limiting case it may be necessary to rely on just one year's data prior to the incident as the baseline of reference, but a longer series covering the period both before and after the pollution event obviously provides a firmer basis for assessing its impact.

Notes

The narrative that relates to section 6.4.2 is based on a presentation given by David Whitmarsh at a workshop in Florence in 2006 as part of the EU-funded ECASA project. This pertains particularly to Figures 6.4 and 6.5, which subsequently appeared in the final project report (www.ecasa.org.uk).

7
Marine Resource Management and the Problem of Non-market Values

7.1 Introduction

The natural resources of the marine environment provide benefits to society over and above commodities such as fish and aquatic plants, and encompass a range of ecosystem services such as nutrient cycling, natural hazard regulation and non-material 'cultural' values, including recreation and amenity. Such benefits are often associated with particular types of coastal habitat, most prominently mangrove, coral reefs and seagrasses, saltmarsh, sand dunes and shingle ridges (Spurgeon, 1998). How should these be factored into marine resource management? The challenge for managers is that these resources are unpriced, which means that the normal metric for assessing their economic value is absent. This problem was touched on earlier in the book, when discussing how to incorporate external costs and benefits into project appraisal (Chapter 4), and also when considering environmental degradation caused by oil spills (Chapter 6). Valuation is necessary in order to decide how marine environmental assets such as mangrove should be used – and in particular, what weight should be given to their conservation. This chapter reviews the different frameworks of analysis that can be brought to bear in deciding how best to use marine living resources, given their multiple functions, and looks specifically at methodologies for the dealing with non-market values associated with marine environmental assets. We consider both monetary approaches based on willingness to pay (WTP) and non-monetary procedures that involve the derivation of weighted scores. The latter is especially appropriate in situations where stated preference methods such as contingent valuation (CV) are impractical – a problem commonly encountered in developing countries – and where the overriding requirement is to establish a preference ranking from key stakeholders about the priorities attached to different policy objectives. These might include environmental protection, but there will generally be others (e.g. fisheries development and its associated benefits of food security and employment creation) which may well conflict with the need to protect the marine environment. Multi-criteria analysis (MCA) is a useful framework for dealing with this kind of trade-off, and has been widely applied in natural resource management. MCA may be more appropriate than cost-benefit analysis (CBA) where decision-makers are concerned with objectives other than maximizing economic efficiency, and this again is a particular characteristic of marine resource management in developing countries.

7.2 Socio-economic appraisal of marine environmental change

7.2.1 Frameworks of analysis

Policy interventions that impact on the marine environment can be evaluated in any one of three ways, each of which provides a formal procedure to enable decision-makers to choose between different management options. A summary of these three approaches is given in Table 7.1, and below we consider the specific problems involved in applying them in a marine context. To make the discussion more concrete, envisage a scenario in which a management authority is looking for ways to rehabilitate a coastal area in which seagrass beds have been degraded through trawling activity, and is considering the creation of a marine protected area (MPA) in the locations where seagrass beds are most vulnerable. At the same time, however, the authority is mindful that such a move would impact on local fisheries and possibly jeopardize livelihoods and food security, at least in the short run. How can such a trade-off be evaluated?

7.2.2 Cost-benefit analysis (CBA)

CBA attempts to quantify the benefits and costs of different policy measures ('projects') in monetary terms, and applies a decision criterion (net present value) to select the option which is expected to produce the highest net benefit to society. If NPV is positive, it implies that the discounted value of benefits exceeds costs, and the project is considered worthwhile. The key requirement in applying the cost-benefit approach to fisheries management, therefore, is the monetary valuation of the effects of different policy options. In the example considered here, the main economic benefit of an MPA is likely to be the economic value of the restored seagrass, while the costs would cover a number of items including not only monitoring and enforcement within the exclusion zone, but also the opportunity cost of short-run losses in fisheries production as a result of

Table 7.1 *Socio-economic assessment of policy and project interventions*

Type of assessment	Purpose and rationale	Requirements and limitations
Cost-benefit analysis	To determine the net economic value of alternative policy and project options, given the aim of maximizing economic efficiency.	Requires monetary values to be attached to all benefits and costs, which may be impossible for many types of environmental impact.
		Because it focuses only on economic efficiency, distributional effects (i.e. winners and losers) have to be dealt with separately.
Cost-effectiveness analysis	To determine the least-cost policy or project option for achieving a defined non-monetary objective (e.g. coastal rehabilitation).	Assumes that different policy and project options are equivalent in terms of impact and outcome.
		Does not measure the economic value of benefits, and so ignores the possibility that none of the options (including the least-cost) may be worthwhile.
Multi-criteria analysis	To determine the 'best' policy or project option in situations involving multiple outcomes that cannot be easily monetized.	Involves the construction of a utility function to prioritize options, but this is often based on expert opinion of only a limited number of stakeholders.
		Scores are relative, not absolute, and are meaningful only to the particular decision problem (e.g. habitat protection options) under consideration.

vessel displacement. Applying CBA in this way is likely to run into several practical difficulties, however. Firstly, as we have already suggested, ecosystem services derived from coastal habitat such as seagrass are difficult to quantify in monetary terms, since they are generally not commercially traded and thus do not command a market price. We explain below some of the ways in which this problem can be addressed, but it remains an inconvenient truth that economic valuation of environmental impacts is not always feasible. Secondly, the effects of an MPA on the benefits of fisheries production is complicated by the need for a reasonably accurate projection of the time profile of catches into the future. This is because, though an MPA may in the long run permit stock recovery and increased yields outside the exclusion zone (via 'spillover' effects), the immediate effect of excluding vessels is likely to be a reduction in catches. The longer it takes for a fishery to recover, and hence the further away in time the benefits are to materialize, the more critical does discounting (and likewise the choice of discount rate) become. These issues aside, the fundamental point to note about CBA is that policy interventions are judged from the standpoint of economic efficiency, the focus being on aggregate net benefits rather than on the welfare of individual groups. In practice, all interventions have equity (i.e. distributional) effects, and in the example considered here it is easy to see how a plan that excludes fishermen from traditional grounds will make them worse off. The significance of this can be tested using sensitivity analysis in which different weights are attached to benefits and costs for the various stakeholder groups. Where the concern is with the welfare of individual groups, either CBA needs to be adapted to explicitly consider the gains and losses to affected parties (Holland et al, 2010), or a completely different framework of analysis should be adopted.

7.2.3 Cost-effectiveness analysis (CEA)

CEA is appropriate where a policy or project has a predefined environmental objective or target, and the aim is to seek out the least-cost way of achieving it if more than one option is available. Though based on an economic efficiency criterion, CEA differs from CBA in that the project benefits are not measured in monetary units. In our MPA example, the main purpose of the intervention is assumed to be coastal rehabilitation via the protection of seagrass from trawl damage, which in a CEA framework might appropriately be specified in terms of a certain hectarage of seagrass to be restored within a given period. One of the main advantages of CEA is that it compels decision-makers to review all available options for meeting an environmental goal, a process that may well be driven by political pressure if the original project is discovered to be more costly than anticipated, or not within budget. In the case of seagrass restoration, the options may in practice be quite limited, and centre on aspects such as MPA configuration (e.g. one single large exclusion zone versus several small) and the method of fisheries enforcement (e.g. regular monitoring versus physical anti-trawling devices). Pickering et al (1999) highlight a particular limitation of CEA in the context of coastal rehabilitation; namely, that different project options are unlikely to be equivalent in terms of their impact on other aspects of environmental quality, even where they are comparable in terms of seagrass restoration. They give the example of artificial reefs, man-made structures which when used as anti-trawling devices may have a positive effect on species biodiversity by acting as a hard substrate for colonization and also encouraging fish assemblage. As such, these structures potentially fulfil an important conservation role that is separate and additional to that achieved from the simple imposition of a trawl ban. A straight comparison of these two options in terms of their cost-effectiveness at protecting seagrass from trawling is thus complicated by the need to account for their impact on species biodiversity. However, arguably the main drawback to CEA is implicit in the method: since it does not attempt to value the outcome of policy interventions in monetary terms, there is no way in which a comparison can be made against costs so as to judge whether the environmental objective or standard in itself is of any social worth (Turner and Adger, 1996). So long as that limitation is recognized, CEA is a useful approach in situations where there is a reasonable consensus of support for a particular policy goal and the possibility that other projects (including environmental) might have a better claim on the resources involved can be dismissed.

7.2.4 Multi-criteria analysis (MCA)

MCA is commonly used when dealing with decision problems involving multiple objectives and trade-offs, a situation that well describes fisheries management where improved performance on one objective (e.g. maximizing resource rent) typically implies a sacrifice elsewhere (e.g. job losses amongst fishermen). Where the challenge is to select the best management strategy, not only must these trade-offs be evaluated, but so too must the effectiveness of the various policy options in achieving each of the different objectives. MCA is especially appropriate where policy interventions have impacts which are difficult to measure in monetary terms, and consequently cost-benefit analysis cannot sensibly be applied. It is also relevant where the concern is not simply with choosing the option that maximizes economic efficiency, but also with the social implications of decisions and their significance for particular stakeholder groups (Brown et al, 2001; Himes, 2007). Indeed, it is because of the need to satisfy the often opposed interests of stakeholders that an understanding of the trade-offs between objectives becomes paramount, since the impact of policy intervention will not fall equally on all groups

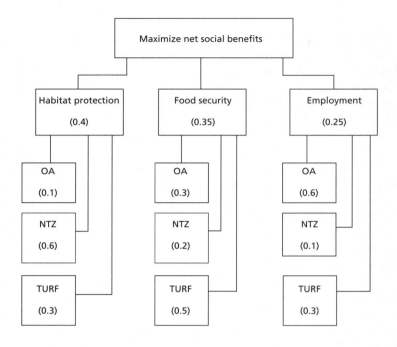

Option	Weight/Score	Habitat	Food security	Employment	Overall
	W =	0.4	0.35	0.25	
Open access	S =	0.1	0.3	0.6	0.295
NTZ	S =	0.6	0.2	0.1	0.335
TURF	S =	0.3	0.5	0.3	0.370

Figure 7.1 *Multi-criteria analysis (MCA) applied to marine resource management: an illustrative example*

(Mardle et al, 2004). Decision problems using MCA are often structured as a hierarchy showing the different criteria and options, and this can be illustrated using our coastal rehabilitation example. Suppose that a management authority in a developing country is concerned with maximizing net social benefits from its marine resources, and wishes to find an appropriate balance between environmental and socio-economic goals. The former is specified in terms of the need to protect submerged aquatic habitat from trawler damage, and the latter in terms of ensuring food security and maintaining employment derived from the locally important artisanal fishery. The management options are given as: (i) open access, under which there is no spatial partitioning and fishing is unrestricted (the status quo baseline); (ii) a pure no-take zone (NTZ) in which no fishing is permitted; (iii) a territorial user right in fishing (TURF) awarded to artisanal boats within an MPA from which trawlers are excluded. The problem is to choose the best management instrument, recognizing that the choice involves a trade-off (i.e. one instrument might perform more effectively on one criterion than another). The decision hierarchy for this hypothetical fishery is summarized in Figure 7.1. If the aim is to come up with a single metric that defines the 'best' option, the MCA process can be summarized in the following steps:

- scoring the options (i.e. assessing the consequences of each management instrument against each criterion);
- weighting the criteria (i.e. assessing their relative importance within the overall goal of marine resource management);
- deriving an overall value and ranking by combining the scores and weights for each option.

Figure 7.1 presents some illustrative figures to show how the decision is reached. In this example, the TURF option ranks highest, followed by the NTZ and lastly the status quo baseline of open access. The point to note is that this result would obviously have been different if a higher weight had been given (say) to habitat protection, the criterion against which NTZ performs best, than to food security, which is most effectively accomplished by having a TURF. The way weights and scores can be obtained in practice is considered in the next section.

7.3 Benefit assessment and the role of monetary valuation

The three approaches described above are all concerned with assessing the net benefits of a proposed intervention in relation to alternative policy or project options. Benefit assessment involves evaluating people's preferences for different outcomes, but this immediately confronts us with the question of how such preferences are articulated and whose values count. The traditional solution to the first of these is to use the concept of willingness to pay (WTP), and this indeed is the rationale underlying CBA and its use of monetary values to assess benefits and costs. Table 7.2 summarizes the main approaches to valuing the marine environment in monetary terms, including a brief description of what each method involves and examples of their application. A number of points can be made in relation to this table.

Firstly, it is clear that the methods can be applied not just to the valuation of fisheries, but potentially at least to a whole range of socially beneficial functions supported by the marine environment. These include recreation and tourism, seascape and visual amenity, water quality and

Table 7.2 *Methodologies for valuing the marine environment*

Method	Description	Example
Bioeconomic models	Examines the interactions between the fish population and the harvesting activity of commercial vessels, so as to identify key reference points for the fishery.	Resource rent in commercial fisheries evaluated from catch and effort data under alternative management scenarios.
Production function models	Obtains an implicit value of a marine resource by measuring its contribution to productive output, which is then monetized using market or surrogate prices.	Indirect use value of coastal habitat (e.g. coral) in supporting offshore fisheries evaluated from productivity data.
Financial analysis	Assesses the financial performance of a representative fishing enterprise under different operating conditions using cost and earnings survey data.	Effect on fish farm profitability following environmental perturbation (e.g. reductions in smolt survival rates).
Expenditure analysis	Estimates patterns of expenditure for the marketed products of marine activity (e.g. fish, boat trips) based on participant survey data.	Tourist expenditure on marine wildlife (e.g. viewing whale sharks) at different stock levels.
Mitigative behaviour	Values environmental quality based on avertive expenditure and/or insurance costs to offset the effects of hazardous events (e.g. declines in water purity).	Value of water quality inferred from compensatory investment by shellfish farms (e.g. purification and relaying).

Method	Description	Example
Hedonic pricing	Values the importance of specific environmental characteristics by assessing their contribution to the observed price of a multi-attribute good (typically property).	Marine environmental quality differences (e.g. in visual amenity) inferred from house-price premia.
Travel cost	Values the recreational benefits of a site based on numbers of visitors, distance travelled and the opportunity cost of the trip.	Recreational benefits of a site (e.g. marine park) inferred from visitor numbers and travel costs.
Contingent valuation	Survey method for constructing a hypothetical market to elicit from respondents their willingness to pay for changes in environmental quality.	Coastal conservation quality derived from stated preference survey of WTP for maintenance of coastal area.
Choice modelling	Survey method for eliciting preferences and deriving implicit prices for environmental attributes based on alternative choice sets or scenarios.	MPA objectives, including habitat protection (e.g. coral) evaluated from stated preferences for alternative policy options.

coastal conservation. Fisheries may co-exist with these functions, and may indeed in some instances be supported by them (e.g. habitat protection and the maintenance of biodiversity), but we should recognize that conflicts may arise, and in such cases the challenge is not just to assess the value of the different activities but also the trade-offs. Cage aquaculture, for example, may lower water quality through organic pollution and possibly intrude on the landscape. Secondly, in most practical applications, our interest is in finding out how economic value would change as a consequence of a modification in the state of the marine environment or in the availability of some critical resource. As Holland et al (2010) have emphasized, it is *incremental* (i.e. marginal) value rather than total value that is important, a point that many politicians often overlook in their concern for big numbers. The question 'what is the total value of this fishery?' is not particularly meaningful, if the implicit alternative is the fairly unrealistic scenario of having no fishery at all and no activity to substitute for it. On the other hand, to enquire how the value of the fishery might increase as a result of (say) a stock enhancement programme involving the release of a specified number of juveniles at least has some operational relevance.

Some of the methods listed in Table 7.2 have already been encountered earlier in the book, and include bioeconomic models of commercial fisheries, as well as more narrowly focused applications such as financial analysis. Because fisheries products are traded, it is legitimate to use market prices as the basis of valuation, where the variable of interest may be resource rent or profit. Bioeconomic models are part of a more generalized approach to valuation, which treats the natural resource as an input into a productive system (e.g. a fishery), and then attempts to estimate the physical relationship between the resource and the resulting output. As applied to fisheries, production function models have been used to establish linkages between environmental inputs such as critical habitat (e.g. wetland) and harvested output (Lynne et al, 1981; Ellis and Fisher, 1987; Farber and Costanza, 1987; Bell, 1989; Freeman, 1991; Barbier and Strand, 1998; Barbier, 2000 and 2003). Here too it is possible to take advantage of market prices, albeit indirectly, because if the marginal productivity of a given area of habitat can be estimated and the value of the product itself (e.g. the price of a tonne of fish) is known, one can then derive an implicit value for the resource itself. Market-based methods of valuation can also be applied to non-fisheries commercial activities such as marine tourism, a good example of which is the use of expenditure analysis to assess the regional economic importance of whale-shark tours in Western Australia (Catlin et al, 2010). The valuation problem may in some circumstances be tackled from the cost side by observing the steps taken to offset or mitigate the effects of environmental deterioration. An illustration of this is the additional costs incurred by molluscan shellfish growers to offset the problem of poor water quality by investing in facilities such as purification and relaying. Such avertive expenditure is an indirect measure of the value of water quality in supporting production.

Other approaches to valuation put the emphasis on taking explicit account of the preferences of individuals affected by changes in environmental quality. These include what are termed revealed preference methods (e.g. travel cost and hedonic pricing) based on observed market or participant behaviour, and stated preference survey methods (e.g. contingent valuation, choice modelling) based on expressed intentions of how people would behave under hypothetical circumstances. The latter are of particular interest here, because they are the only way in which both use and 'passive' use values can be quantified in monetary terms. The most widely used stated preference method is contingent valuation, which in recent years has been applied to several types of aquatic resource issues, including beach renourishment, water quality improvement, eutrophication reduction, marine mammal preservation, coral reef quality, coastal conservation and wetland habitat protection (Ledoux and Turner, 2002; Remoundou et al, 2009). CVM has also been used as a natural resource damage assessment procedure, arguably the best known such application being that of the *Exxon Valdez* tanker disaster mentioned in the last chapter (MPP-EAS, 1999; Carson et al, 2003). A more recent example of the use of CVM for damage assessment is the study by Loureiro et al (2009) of the valuation of environmental losses caused by the *Prestige* oil spill in 2002/3, which as well as having a serious impact on commercial fisheries also caused extensive pollution to a long stretch of coastline, and harm to sea birds and mammals. The study involved a questionnaire survey of Spanish territories in which respondents were given information about the spill and its environmental impact, and then asked about their willingness to support a programme that would avoid the worst effects of an oil spill of similar size in the future. It was suggested that funding for such a programme would partly come from Spanish taxpayers in the form of a one-time payment, and respondents were accordingly invited to say whether or not they would be willing to pay stated amounts into the proposed fund. Based on the questionnaire responses (1140 in total), the parametric estimate of mean WTP was €40.51 and the total amount aggregated across all Spanish households was €574 million. This figure represents both a prospective assessment of how much people would be prepared to give up to avoid a *Prestige*-type incident in the future, and a retrospective calculation of the actual environmental damages of the spill itself. Of particular interest in the present context is that the figure of €574 million is of a similar order of magnitude to the commercial losses to fisheries and tourism (Loureiro et al, 2009: p552), a fact that illustrates quite neatly why the valuation of non-market environmental assets is important.

7.4 Scoring procedures for assessing environmental attributes

7.4.1 The analytic hierarchy process (AHP)

In our earlier discussion of multi-criteria analysis (MCA), it was suggested that the use of money as a measure of economic value was not always feasible, and this has prompted the use of scoring methods to assess the significance of policy interventions that impact on the marine environment. This has been driven partly by a general dissatisfaction with the ethics of monetary valuation which is seen to commodify the natural environment, but there is now also a well-developed critique of stated preference methods such as CVM which are claimed to produce value estimates of questionable reliability. This is especially the case where survey respondents have no experience of paying for environmental amenities, or else feel uncomfortable in answering direct questions about the monetary value they place on their availability (FAO, 2008a). A related concern is that cost-benefit analysis (CBA) is based on a definition of social welfare that ignores the preferences of particular interest groups, and since policy interventions invariably produce losers as well as winners, it is clear that the whole notion of 'optimality' needs to be redefined. Scoring procedures lend themselves to this challenge, and below we consider their use in a marine context.

One commonly used technique is the analytic hierarchy process (AHP), a multi-criteria assessment method developed by Saaty (1977) that enables qualitative judgements about the relative importance of different objectives to be quantified in commensurable terms. There are a growing number of applications of AHP to decision problems involving marine and aquatic resources, the main areas being fisheries policy (DiNardo et al, 1989; Leung et al, 1998; Soma, 2003; Nielsen and Mathiesen, 2006; Lane, 2007; Utne, 2008; Pascoe et al, 2009a and 2009b), marine aquaculture (Whitmarsh and Wattage, 2006; Halide et al, 2009; Whitmarsh and Palmieri, 2009), fish product quality (Setala et al, 2000; Saarni et al, 2001), recreational site choice (Kangas, 1995; Ramos et al, 2006), marine protected area performance indicators (Himes, 2007), wetland management (Herath, 2004; Wattage and Mardle, 2005 and 2006) and marine environmental impacts (Innes and Pascoe, 2010). In AHP, respondents are asked to make pairwise comparisons between different objectives, where the intensity of preference is measured on a ratio scale (usually nine-point), illustrated in Table 7.3. Responses can be converted to scores to show the weight or priority attached to each objective using a procedure based on the concept of a pairwise comparison matrix, whose elements denote the relative importance of one objective vis-a-vis another. For a matrix with n objectives, there will be 0.5n[n−1] pairwise comparisons.

Table 7.3 *Pairwise comparison scheme used in AHP*

Pairwise comparison	Relative importance	
	Verbal description	Numeric scale
	Extreme	9
		8
Objective A	Very strong	7
compared to		6
objective B	Strong	5
		4
	Moderate	3
		2
	Equal	1
		2
	Moderate	3
Objective B		4
compared to	Strong	5
objective A		6
	Very strong	7
		8
	Extreme	9

7.4.2 Putting AHP into practice

To illustrate how AHP works, consider a situation where a management authority is establishing a set of objectives for a fishery and wishes to find out from the main stakeholder groups where their preferences lie. Following discussion, the objectives are agreed to be:

- maximize self-sufficiency in locally-sourced fish supplies;
- maximize foreign exchange earnings from access fees;
- maximize income in the catching and onshore sectors;
- minimize conflicts with other coastal zone users;
- minimize marine habitat damage.

Figure 7.2 shows how one respondent may have prioritized these objectives, with the results presented in the format of a pairwise comparison matrix using the 1 to 9 scale. Since $n = 5$, there will be $0.5n[n-1] = 10$ pairwise comparisons. The upper part of the figure indicates that data only need to be obtained on the top right-hand corner of the matrix, since the bottom left-hand corner is assumed to be reciprocal. What this means is that, if the respondent has indicated that self-sufficiency is rated as 'extremely important' (= 9) in relation to foreign exchange, the logical corollary is that the reciprocal relationship (1/9) should express the

	Self-sufficiency	Foreign exchange	Income	User conflict	Habitat damage	Geometric mean	Normalized GM
Self-sufficiency	1	•	•	•	•		
Foreign exchange		1	•	•	•		
Income			1	•	•		
User conflict				1	•		
Habitat damage					1		

	Self-sufficiency	Foreign exchange	Income	User conflict	Habitat damage	Geometric mean	Normalized GM
Self-sufficiency	1	9	1	7	3	2.85	0.41
Foreign exchange	1/9	1	1/7	1	1/5	0.32	0.05
Income	1	7	1	4	1	1.95	0.28
User conflict	1/7	1	1/4	1	1/3	0.41	0.06
Habitat damage	1/3	5	1	3	1	1.38	0.2
						6.91	1.00

Figure 7.2 *AHP pairwise comparison matrix and illustrative data*

view that foreign exchange is extremely unimportant relative to self-sufficiency. The recommended method for obtaining the overall priority weights from these scores is based on the calculation of what is known in mathematics as the principal right eigenvector of the matrix (Saaty, 1977), but a widely used approximation to this can be derived from the normalized row geometric mean. Using this method, for our single respondent the weights in rank order come out as self-sufficiency (41 per cent), income (28 per cent), habitat protection (20 per cent), user conflict (6 per cent) and foreign exchange (5 per cent).

In many practical applications of AHP, the preferences and choices of a particular group may require data from several respondents if one is not considered to be representative. This would be true, for example, where a sectional interest such as the 'green' lobby is made up of a number of separate organizations. Indeed, one of the advantages of AHP is that it can help highlight similarities and differences in attitudes between individuals who may ostensibly be part of the same stakeholder group, and to do so might be considered a necessary check before any collective average of priority weights is calculated. In the past few years AHP has also been used to elicit preferences from the community at large, an application which seems quite appropriate where the aim is to see how far public attitudes are congruent with those of stakeholder groups whose involvement with the political process is necessarily partisan. This scaling-up from group to community level effectively turns AHP into a social survey methodology, and accordingly close attention needs to be paid to the statistical requirements of sampling design in order to ensure validity and reliability. A further technical issue relates to the fact that individual respondents are hardly ever perfectly consistent in their pairwise choices, and a judgement thus has to be made about the degree of inconsistency that is acceptable in the responses. A commonly used measure is based on the Consistency Index (CI), calculated as:

$$CI = [\lambda_{max} - n] / [n-1]$$

where λ_{max} is the maximum eigenvalue of the pairwise comparison matrix [A] and n is the number of objectives. A Consistency Ratio (CR) can be derived from this, such that:

$$CR = CI/RI$$

where RI is a randomly generated index.

Higher values of CR indicate greater inconsistency in responses, and a common rule of thumb (Saaty and Vargas, 2000) is to exclude cases where the CR > 0.1. It should be stressed, however, that this threshold is arbitrary, and it may reasonably be argued that in AHP surveys of public preferences, all responses are valid in their own terms and should be retained in the dataset, even where they fail to meet the inconsistency test.

The discussion so far has centred on the use of AHP in eliciting preferences for different management objectives, and for decision problems involving marine resources this is arguably its major strength. But as we saw earlier, multi-criteria analysis (MCA) also requires a knowledge of the impact or effectiveness of different options for achieving the various objectives, and it is questionable whether AHP is the best method to achieve this. One of the weaknesses with AHP, as recently pointed out by Pascoe et al (2009), is that it fails to identify negative impacts that follow from policy intervention. Awarding territorial user rights (TURFs) to indigenous fishermen, for example, may increase self-sufficiency in locally caught fish supply, but worsen habitat damage if it results in intensified fishing pressure. To deal with this kind of trade-off, Pascoe et al recommend using a scale that ranges from +1 to +3 for positive impacts and −1 to −3 for negative impacts, with zero corresponding to no change. Higher absolute values indicate greater severity, shown in Table 7.4, so that, for example, a management measure that is anticipated to cause a 'large increase' in one objective and a 'moderate decline' in another would be rated as +3 and −2 respectively. The judgements underpinning the impacts would be obtained from expert opinion, but as Pascoe et al explain, these may be informed by quantitative assessments such as bioeconomic models. These numeric values can then be multiplied by the weights attached to the various objectives to generate an overall measure of whether a policy intervention results in a net improvement or deterioration relative to the status quo baseline.

Table 7.4 *Scale for assessing impacts of policy intervention*

Scale	Effect	Description
+3		Large increase
+2	Positive	Moderate increase
+1		Some increase
0		No change
−1		Some decline
−2	Negative	Moderate decline
−3		Large decline

Source: Based on Pascoe et al (2009)

7.4.3 Case study: the environmental performance of salmon aquaculture

In the first chapter we discussed the important role of aquaculture in world supplies, but pointed out also the growing concerns over its sustainability. Cage aquaculture in particular has a controversial environmental record and from a policy standpoint it is important to know how people perceive this issue and what weight should be attached to it in planning the development of the industry. Salmon farming in Scotland illustrates clearly some of the trade-offs involved, since it has not only produced positive socio-economic benefits, by creating jobs in areas where employment opportunities are limited, but has also in a variety of ways impacted negatively on the marine environment. AHP has been used in two public attitude surveys of Scottish salmon farming, the main result in both cases being that people exhibit a measurable degree of concern for the sustainability of the industry and implicitly accept that improved environmental performance may necessitate a sacrifice in terms of other objectives.

In the first of the studies, Whitmarsh and Wattage (2006) administered a postal questionnaire to Scottish households in which AHP was used to elicit priority weights for five performance indicators, which included the minimization of environmental damages (e.g. pollution and disease) caused by salmon farms. Parallel to this was a CVM question in which respondents were asked whether, and by how much, they would be willing to pay extra for salmon that had been farmed using a production method that resulted in half the amount of organic pollution. The survey indicated that on average people were willing to pay a premium of some 22 per cent over the price of conventional salmon, but of particular interest was the finding that the variation in WTP responses could be partly explained by people's environmental preferences, as measured by their AHP priority weights. In other words, the greater the importance that individuals attached to minimizing environmental damage from salmon farming, the higher the price premium that they would be willing to pay for salmon that had been farmed more sustainably. Evidence that the Scottish public are not indifferent to the environmental performance of salmon farming is confirmed by the second of the studies (Whitmarsh and Palmieri, 2009), which likewise used AHP to elicit public and stakeholder attitudes towards the industry. A hierarchy of objectives was developed in which a distinction was made at one level between maximizing socio-economic benefits and minimizing environmental damage, and at the next level between a set of more specific constituent criteria: (i) employment and livelihoods; (ii) edible supplies of fish; (iii) tax contribution; (iv) pollution and water quality; (v) visual intrusion and landscape impacts; and (vi) impact on wild salmon stocks. Postal questionnaires were administered to a sample of residents in five coastal regions covering mainland Scotland (Argyll & Bute, and the Highlands) and the offshore areas (Orkney, Shetland and the Western Isles), while a separate AHP survey of stakeholders representing key interest groups was also conducted. Here we will focus on the results of the public attitude survey in order to illustrate one of the main sets of findings, which were the regional differences in community preferences regarding salmon farming and its environmental performance. These are illustrated in Figure 7.3, which for each of the coastal areas shows the priority weights attached to the environmental criteria. In four of the five regions, the weights exceed 50 per cent, implying that somewhat greater importance was attached to the objective of minimizing environmental damage than to the maximization of socio-economic benefits.

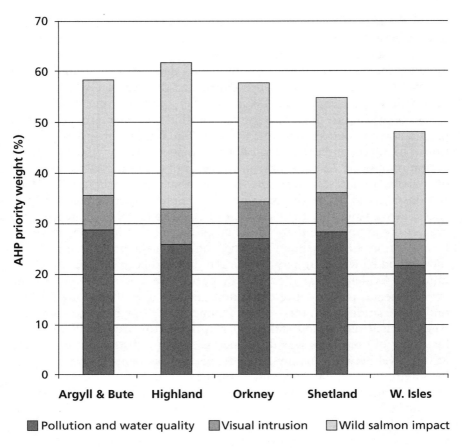

Pollution and water quality ▨Visual intrusion ☐Wild salmon impact

Source: Constructed from data given in Whitmarsh and Palmieri (2009)

Figure 7.3 *Community preferences for minimizing environmental impacts of Scottish salmon farming*

7.5 Conclusion

The material covered in this final chapter brings together many of the ideas explored throughout the book, a central theme being the question of how to incorporate non-market values into marine resource management. The problem goes right to the heart of economics, which as we explained at the beginning is concerned with the implications of scarcity. Here we have been mostly concerned with ecosystem services supplied by the marine environment, whose true scarcity is concealed by the fact that the normal mechanism for signalling their value to society is missing – such services are generally not bought and sold in the market place, and are quite literally 'priceless'. The familiar consequence of this is that resources become mis-used, since they are treated as a free gift of nature, but it also presents a broader challenge of deciding how these resources should be managed. The argument put forward here is that management requires valuation, where the 'values' that underlie the process can be defined as the 'beliefs, either individual or social, about what is important in life and thus about the ends or objectives which should govern public policies' (Royal Commission on Environmental Pollution, 1998). In many circumstances it may be appropriate to use monetary values to assess the importance of the marine environment, but experience suggests that this is by no means a straightforward exercise, especially where stated preference techniques such as CVM need to be applied in order to find out from people their willingness to pay. The fact remains, however, that choices have to be made. Where monetary valuation is not feasible, some alternative way needs to be found for people to articulate their beliefs about what is important in the use of the marine environment. This is where preference elicitation methods such as AHP have much to commend them, since they are not only relatively simple to use, but also enable policy-makers to confront the question 'whose values count?' when applied to separate stakeholder groups.

Appendix A
Estimating Maximum Fisheries Production Using Time Series Data

The constraints facing capture fisheries against a backdrop of increasing food demand make it important to be able to estimate potential catches and their state of exploitation. A simple method for doing this has been developed by Grainger and Garcia (1996), based on a generalized fishery model using time series data for defined sea areas and regions. The model is based on the assumption that fisheries develop through four stages, defined as: (i) undeveloped; (ii) developed; (iii) mature; (iv) senescent. To operationalize the model, it is necessary to have a reasonably long series of catch observations in order to chart the changes in the annual rate of growth which occur throughout these stages.

To illustrate the method, we will use the Eastern Central Atlantic (CECAF 34) region, whose marine resources support the fisheries of neighbouring African coastal states and a number of distant water fleets. The basic relationships are given as:

$$[C_{t+1} - C_t] / C_t = a + bT$$

where:

C = catch
T = time (years)
a and b are parameters to be estimated
t-subscripts refer to years

Maximum production according to the model is the value corresponding to the year when the relative rate of catch increase (RRCI) is zero. In their analysis, Grainger and Garcia smooth the data using a three-year running average such that RRCI is estimated as:

$$\text{RRCI} = [C_t - (C_t + C_{t-1} + C_{t-2}) / 3] / [(C_t + C_{t-1} + C_{t-2}) / 3]$$
$$= a + bT \qquad \qquad \text{(Equation 1)}$$

Maximum production can be found by taking the estimated parameters and fitting them to the equation:

$$C_{t+1} = C_t [a + bT + 1] \qquad \qquad \text{(Equation 2)}$$

FAO data for CECAF 34 are available from the 1950s, and here include all aquatic plants and animals excluding marine mammals. The graph of RRCI and the linear trend fitted using Equation 1 (Figure A1) implies that the fisheries were no longer expanding by 1996, and in the following years the growth rate was negative. This is confirmed by the corresponding graph (Figure A2) of total catch and fitted production based on Equation 2, showing that harvest potential had reached its limit in the mid-1990s, at a maximum estimated production of some 4 million tonnes per annum.

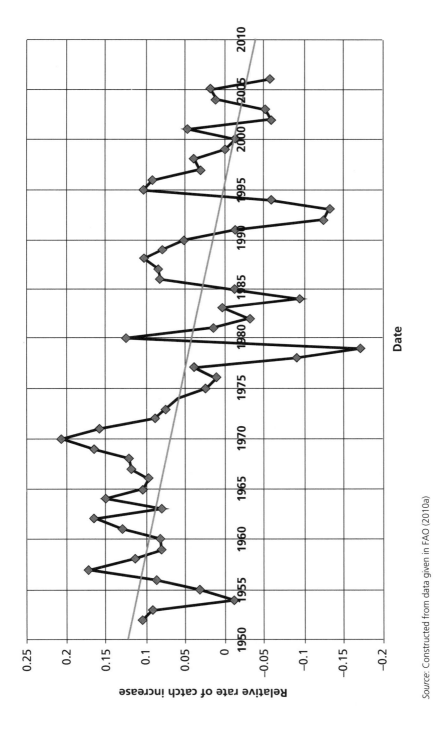

Source: Constructed from data given in FAO (2010a)

Figure A1 *Catches in Eastern Central Atlantic (CECAF 34): trend in annual relative rate of increase in landings*

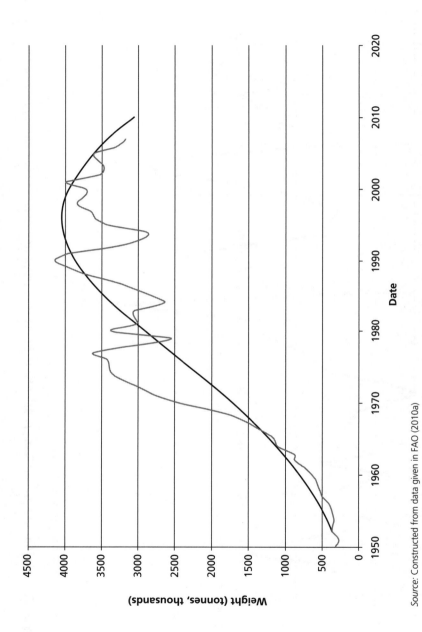

Source: Constructed from data given in FAO (2010a)

Figure A2 *Catches in Eastern Central Atlantic (CECAF 34): actual and fitted values for weight of landings*

Appendix B
Bioeconomic Analysis and Fisheries Management

Introduction

Here we outline the main elements of the simple static Gordon-Schaefer bioeconomic model, given a common pool resource where movement of effort into or out of the fishery is driven by profit expectations. Note that even though fishermen may incur charges (or alternatively be in receipt of subsidies, which are negative charges), these are classed as a 'transfer payment' and thus do not enter into the calculation of economic rent. The latter is defined as the difference between the value of output from the fishery and the opportunity cost of the inputs needed to produce it. However, because charges and subsidies impact directly on the financial profits of fishermen, they can be used to regulate fishing activity away from its original open-access position. The model here considers the case of a fishery where a charge is levied on fishing effort, so fishermen are required to pay €X per day at sea. In theory it can be shown that charges can be used to extract the greatest amount of economic rent from the fishery. This management reference point is defined as maximum economic yield.

Definitions and symbols

Quantity	Symbol	Typical units
Sustainable yield	Y	Tonnes
Fishing effort	E	Standard vessel-days
Total charge receipts	T	€
Total financial profit	Π	€
Catch per unit of effort	U	Tonnes per standard vessel-day
Economic rent	R	€
Cost per unit of effort	c	€ per standard vessel-day

Charge rate	t	€ per standard vessel-day
Price of fish	p	€ per tonne of fish
Catchability coefficient	q	Tonnes per vessel-day per unit of stock
Intrinsic growth rate of the fish stock	r	Percentage per year
Environmental carrying capacity	L	Tonnes

Key functional relationships

Variable	Relationship with fishing effort
Y	$= qLE - (q^2LE^2) / r$
T	$= tE$
Π	$= p[qLE - (q^2LE^2) / r] - cE - tE$
U	$= qL - (q^2LE) / r$
R	$= p[qLE - (q^2LE^2) / r] - cE$

Fisheries management reference points with respect to effort

Reference point	Abbreviation	Formula
Open access	E_{oa}	$= r[pqL - (c+t)] / pq^2L$
MSY	E_{msy}	$= r / 2q$
MEY	E_{mey}	$= r(pqL - c) / 2pq^2L$

Example

Consider a fishery whose biological and economic characteristics are defined by the following baseline parameter values:

Cost per unit of effort (c)	$= 1750$
Charge rate (t)	$= 0$
Price (p)	$= 1000$
Catchability coefficient (q)	$= 0.000025$
Intrinsic growth rate (r)	$= 0.25$
Environmental carrying capacity (L)	$= 250,000$

The fishery is open access and, initially, no charges are levied on fishermen. Suppose now that the management authority wishes to use charges to reduce effort, and move the fishery nearer to what it considers a more appropriate level such as MSY or MEY. Given the parameter values, we can use the formulae above to work out what the optimal charge rate needs to be to achieve either of these target reference points. The simplest way to do this is to first derive the effort levels for OA, MSY and MSY and then substitute the result into whichever of the functional relationship equations (e.g. yield, rent, charge receipts, CPUE) is of interest. This will produce the following results:

Performance indicator	Baseline	MSY strategy	MEY strategy
	t = 0	t = 1375	t = 2250
E_{oa}	7200	5000	3600
E_{msy}	5000	5000	5000
E_{mey}	3600	3600	3600
Y_{oa}	12,600	15,625	14,400
Y_{msy}	15,625	15,625	15,625
Y_{mey}	14,400	14,400	14,400
U_{oa}	1.75	3.13	4.00
T_{oa}	0	6,875,000	8,100,100
R_{mey}	8,100,000	8,100,000	8,100,100

Assessment

Because the fishery is assumed to be based on a common-pool resource, imposing charges merely changes its character from one of unregulated to regulated open access. The tendency will still be for profit to be competed away if revenue exceeds cost, but the prospect of having to pay an additional charge on top of normal operating costs will force some fishermen to quit. In other words, charges shift the original open-access equilibrium to a lower effort level. The GS model can be used to demonstrate the implications of such a move and the trade-offs involved. The following points should be noted:

(i) In the unregulated baseline state, the level of effort at open access (7200) is exactly double that at MEY (3600). The economic rent is fully dissipated, whereas if effort had been managed at the MEY level it could generate €8.1 million. This potential source of wealth is also lost to the management authorities, since by assumption the mechanism by which the rent could be appropriated (charges) is non-operational.

(ii) If the management objective is MSY, this can be achieved with a charge rate of €1375 per unit of effort. Effort is reduced to 5000 days, with a corresponding rise in sustainable yield from 12,600 to 15,625 tonnes. The management authorities succeed in capturing a substantial proportion (€6.875 million) of the potential maximum economic rent via charge receipts.

(iii) Where MEY is the objective, a charge rate of €2250 per day is warranted. This will reduce effort to 3600 days, and the charge receipts of €8.1 million will now equate exactly with the MEY rent level. Yield at 14,400 tonnes is higher than its original baseline level of 12,600 tonnes, but this by definition is less than that attainable at MSY (15,625). Accordingly, there is a trade-off between these alternative objectives: maximizing economic rent does not maximize physical catch.

(iv) The financial effects of these changes on the fishermen who remain in the fishery are ambiguous. The model shows that CPUE is 1.75 tonnes per day at the original open-access (charge rate = 0), 3.13 tonnes per day at MSY (charge rate = 1375) and 4.00 tonnes per day at MEY (charge rate = 2250). This implies that, while they lose by having to pay the effort charge, they can expect to gain in the long run (once the fish stock has adjusted to reduced pressure of harvesting) from higher catch rates.

Appendix C
Estimating Resource Rent Based on Surplus Production Models

In a study of the Western Hawaiian Islands lobster fishery, Clarke, Yoshimoto and Pooley (1992) outline a method for estimating a surplus production model using catch and effort data. Like the model developed by Fox (1970), the CYP model is based on the assumption that the growth of the fish stock can be described mathematically by a Gompertz growth function, having the specification:

$$Y = q.K.E.exp^{-(q/r)E} \qquad \text{(I)}$$

where:

Y = Yield
E = Effort
q = Catchability coefficient
K = Environmental carrying capacity
r = Intrinsic growth rate of the stock

For data on yield and effort, the challenge is then to estimate q, K and r. The estimating equation proposed by CYP uses annual observations on catch per unit of effort (CPUE), such that:

$$\ln[U_t] = b_0 + b_1 \ln[U_{t-1}] + b_2 [E_t + E_{t-1}] \qquad \text{(II)}$$

where:

U = Catch per unit of effort (CPUE)
$\ln[U_t]$ = natural logarithm of CPUE in the current year (t)
$\ln[U_{t-1}]$ = natural logarithm of CPUE in the previous year (t–1)
$[E_t + E_{t-1}]$ = Sum of effort in the current and previous year

Clarke et al show that the parameters b_0, b_1 and b_2 in Equation II are related to the constant terms (r, q and K) in Equation I as follows:

$$r = (2 - 2b_1) / (1 + b_1) \tag{III}$$
$$q = -b_2(2 + r) \tag{IV}$$
$$K = \exp[((2 + r)b_0)/2r] / q \tag{V}$$

Reference points for MSY and open-access in this model are uniquely defined as:

$$Y_{msy} = (qK) / [(q/r) * \exp(1)] \tag{VI}$$
$$E_{msy} = r/q \tag{VII}$$
$$E_{oa} = r [\ln(qK) - \ln(c/p)] / q \tag{VIII}$$

where:

c = cost per unit cost of effort
p = price of fish

Equation II can be estimated using multiple regression. There are currently many user-friendly computer software packages that include regression analysis, and one of the most suitable for this purpose is SPSS for Windows. This program also features some important diagnostic tests for judging the statistical reliability of the model that are not to be found in spreadsheets such as Microsoft Excel, and for any fisheries research that is intended for publication such tests would normally be required. However, for the purpose of showing how to obtain a fitted yield curve from catch and effort data, Excel is entirely appropriate and we will apply it here to the Maldivian data given in Chapter 2. The data to be used in Equation II might appear in part of the Excel worksheet, as shown in Figure C1.

The first column is the natural logarithm of CPUE, and the second column is the same data lagged one year. The third column is simply the sum of effort over a two-year period. The regression routine in Excel requires us to specify the dependent variable (column 1) and the independent variables (columns 2 and 3).

These results show that the data provides quite a good overall fit to the model ($R^2 = 0.868$, $F = 29.1$), and importantly the regression coefficients on the two independent variables (X1 and X2) are both statistically significant. Based on these estimates, therefore, the parameters of Equation II can be given as:

$b_0 = 0.0405$
$b_1 = 0.5035$
$b_2 = -0.0000006590$

lnU_t	lnU_{t-1}	$[E_t + E_{t+1}]$
−0.422		
−0.436	−0.422	184,657
−0.380	−0.436	173,861
−0.116	−0.380	162,853
−0.006	−0.116	151,185
−0.023	−0.006	149,280
−0.023	−0.023	160,703
−0.075	−0.023	170,690
−0.106	−0.075	187,949
−0.069	−0.106	211,262
−0.203	−0.069	239,616
−0.282	−0.203	267,946
−0.432	−0.282	296,531
−0.359	−0.432	321,546
−0.362	−0.359	341,857
−0.549	−0.362	376,984
−0.623	−0.549	433,032
−0.495	−0.623	495,951
−0.595	−0.495	538,801
−0.607	−0.595	561,546
−0.417	−0.607	563,119
−0.388	−0.417	544,250
−0.749	−0.388	565,092

Figure C1 *Data for use in Equation II*

Accordingly, from Equations III to V, we may then derive:

r = 0.6605
q = 0.000001753
K = 618,791

Substituting these values into Equation I gives the yield curve as:

$$Y = 1.0792E.exp^{(-0.0000007152E)}$$

Using the values suggested by Sinan and Whitmarsh (2010) for the price of fish and the cost of effort (p = 1314, c = 632), the MSY and open-access reference points can be obtained by substituting into Equations VI to VIII to produce:

Y_{msy} = 150,360 tonnes
E_{msy} = 376,733 vessel day-trips
E_{oa} = 306,448 vessel day-trips

SUMMARY OUTPUT

Regression statistics

Multiple R	0.868
R square	0.754
Adjusted R square	0.728
Standard error	0.117
Observations	22

ANOVA

	df	SS	MS	F	Significance F
Regression	2	0.800	0.400	29.122	0.000
Residual	19	0.261	0.014		
Total	21	1.061			

	Coefficients	Standard error	t-stat	P-value	Lower 95%	Upper 95%	Lower 95%	Upper 95%
Intercept	0.0405	0.0576	0.7028	0.4907	−0.0888	0.1610	−0.0800	0.1610
X Variable 1	0.5035	0.1886	2.6692	0.0152	0.1087	0.8983	0.1087	0.8983
X Variable 2	−6.59E-07	0.0000	−2.7000	0.0142	0.0000	0.0000	0.0000	0.0000

Figure C2 *Results of regression analysis*

These results suggest that, given the market and cost conditions prevailing in the Maldivian fisheries in the most recent time period (2007), the open-access equilibrium level of fishing effort was less than that required to harvest the maximum sustainable yield.

Resource rent, which we defined earlier as the difference between the value of the catch and the opportunity cost of the inputs needed to produce it, can now be found straightforwardly. At the open-access effort level of 306,448 vessel day-trips, the resource rent will be zero. This is because at that point the total value of the catch (yield in tonnes multiplied by price per tonne) will exactly equate with total cost (effort multiplied by cost per day-trip). We can show that there is only one level of effort at which resource rent is maximized, and based on our estimated results this is at 136,675 vessel day-trips. At that point, the resource rent is $49.2 million per annum.

References

ACOPS (2008) *Advisory Committee on Protection of the Sea Annual Survey of Reported Discharges Attributed to Vessels and Offshore Oil & Gas Installations Operating in the United Kingdom Pollution Control Zone 2007*, London, ACOPS.

Agnew, D.J. and Barnes, C.T. (2003) *The Economic and Social Effects of IUU/FOC Fishing*, Paris, OECD.

Allison, E.H., Perry, A.L., Badjeck, M.-C. et al (2009) 'Vulnerability of national economies to the impacts of climate change on fisheries', *Fish and Fisheries*, vol 10, no 2, pp1–24.

Al-Mazrooei, N., Chomo, G.V. and Omezzine, A. (2003) 'Purchase behaviour of consumers for seafood products', *Agricultural and Marine Sciences*, vol 8, no 1, pp1–10.

Anderson, D.M. (2009) 'Approaches to monitoring, control and management of harmful algal blooms (HABs)', *Ocean and Coastal Management*, vol 52, pp342–347.

Anderson, J.L. (2007) 'Sustainable aquaculture: What does it mean and how do we get there?', in P.S. Leung, C.-S. Lee and P.J. O'Bryen (eds) *Species and system selection for sustainable aquaculture*, Oxford, Blackwell Publishing, pp9–17.

Anderson, J., Curtis, H., Boyle, R. and Graham, K. (2008) *2005 Economic Survey of the UK Fishing Fleet*, Edinburgh, Sea Fish Industry Authority.

Arnason, R., Hannesson, R. and Schrank, W. (2000) 'Costs of fisheries management: the cases of Iceland, Norway and Newfoundland', *Marine Policy*, vol 24, no 3, pp233–243.

Asche, F. and Bjorndal, T. (2010) 'Aquaculture: Production and Markets', in R.Q. Grafton, R. Hilborn, D, Squires et al (eds) *Handbook of Marine Fisheries Conservation and Management*, Oxford University Press, pp60–71.

Asche, F., Bjorndal, T. and Gordon, D.V. (2007) 'Studies in the Demand Structure for Fish and Seafood Products', in A. Weintraub, C. Romero, T. Bjorndal et al (eds) *Handbook of Operations Research in Natural Resources*, Springer.

Asche, F., Bjorndal, T. and Sissener, E.H. (2003) 'Relative productivity development in salmon aquaculture', *Marine Resource Economics*, vol 18, pp205–210.

Barbier, E.B. (2000) 'Valuing the environment as input: review of applications to mangrove-fishery linkages', *Ecological Economics*, vol 35, pp47–61.

Barbier, E.B. (2003) 'Habitat-fishery linkages and mangrove loss in Thailand', *Contemporary Economic Policy*, vol 21, no 1, pp59–77.

Barbier, E.B. and Strand, I. (1998) 'Valuing mangrove-fishery linkages. A case study of Campeche, Mexico', *Environmental and Resource Economics*, vol 12, pp151–166.

Barde, J.-P. and Pearce, D.W. (eds) (1991) *Valuing the environment: six case studies*, London, Earthscan.

Bartley, D.M. and Leber, K.M. (2004) 'Marine Ranching', FAO Fisheries Technical Paper 429, Rome, FAO.

Bell, F. (1968) 'The Pope and the Price of Fish', *American Economic Review*, vol 50, pp1346–1350.

Bell, F. (1978) *Food from the Sea: the Economics and Politics of Ocean Fisheries*, Boulder, Colorado, Westview Press.

Bell, F.W. (1989) 'Application of wetland valuation theory to commercial and recreational fisheries in Florida', Report No 95, Florida Sea Grant Program, Florida State University.

Bjorndal, T. and Munro, G.R. (1998) 'The Economics of Fisheries Management: A Survey', in T. Tietenburg and H. Folmer (eds) *The International Yearbook of Environmental and Resource Economics 1998/1999: A Survey of Current Issues*, Cheltenham, Edward Elgar, pp153–188.

Black, K.D. (ed.) (2001) *Environmental Impacts of Aquaculture*, Sheffield, Academic Press.

Brander, K.M. (2007) 'Global fish production and climate change', *PNAS*, vol 104, no 50, pp19709–19714.

Brown, K., Adger, W.N., Tompkins, E. et al (2001) 'Trade-off analysis for marine protected area management', *Ecological Economics*, vol 37, pp417–434.

Brown, K., Tompkins, E. and Adger, N. (2002) *Making Waves: Integrating Coastal Conservation and Development*, London, Earthscan.

Caddy, J.F. and Gulland, J.A. (1983) 'Historical patterns of fish stocks', *Marine Policy*, Oct.

Cameron, S. (2005) *Econometrics*, New York, McGraw-Hill Higher Education

Carson, R.T., Mitchell, R.C., Hanemann, M. et al (2003) 'Contingent Valuation and Lost Passive Use: Damages from the Exxon Valdez Oil Spill', *Environmental and Resource Economics*, vol 25, pp257–286.

Catlin, J., Jones, T., Norman, B. and Wood, D. (2010) 'Consolidation in a wildlife tourism industry: the changing impact of whale shark tourist expenditure in the Ningaloo coast region', *International Journal of Tourism Research*, vol 12, pp134–148.

Charles, A. (1992) 'Fishery conflicts: a unified framework', *Marine Policy*, vol 16, no 5, pp379–393.

Charles, A. (2001) *Sustainable Fishery Systems*, Oxford, Blackwell Science.

Clark, C.W. (1985) *Bioeconomic Modelling and Fisheries Management*, Chichester, John Wiley and Sons.

Clarke, R.P., Yoshimoto, S.S. and Pooley, S.G. (1992) 'A Bioeconomic Analysis of the North-Western Hawaiian Islands Lobster Fishery', *Marine Resource Economics*, vol 7, no 2, pp115–140.

Cohen, M. (1995) 'Technological disasters and natural resource damage assessment: an evaluation of the *Exxon Valdez* oil spill', *Land Economics*, vol 71, no 1, pp65–82.

Cohen, M. (2010) 'A Taxonomy of Oil Spill Costs: What are the Likely Costs of the Deepwater Horizon Spill?', Background Paper, Resources for the Future, May 2010.

Collins, A., Pascoe, S. and Whitmarsh, D. (2003) 'Pollution externalities and fisheries: insights from a spatially explicit bioeconomic model', *Marine Resource Economics*, vol 18, no 4, pp313–328.

Cruz-Trinidad, A. (1990) 'The use of surplus-yield models in the economic analysis of a fishery', *Fishbyte*, vol 8, no 2, pp20–24.

Cunningham, S. and Neiland, A. (2005) 'Investigating the linkages between fisheries, poverty and growth: policy brief', Report prepared for the Project 'The role of fisheries in poverty alleviation and growth: past, present and future', Department for International Development.

Cunningham, S., Dunn, M.R. and Whitmarsh, D. (1985) *Fisheries Economics: An Introduction*, Mansell Publishing Ltd.

Cunningham, S., Iyaye, S. and Zeine, D. (2005) 'The Experience of the Mauritanian Fish Trading Company (SMCP) in the Management of the Fisheries Sector in Mauritania', in S. Cunningham and T. Bostock (eds) *Successful Fisheries Management: Issues, Case Studies and Perspectives*, Delft, Eburon.

Cunningham, S., Neiland, A.E., Arbuckle, M. and Bostock, T. (2009) 'Wealth-based fisheries management: using fisheries wealth to orchestrate sound fisheries policy in practice', *Marine Resource Economics*, vol 24, pp271–287.

Daw, T., Adger, W.N., Brown, K. and Badjeck, M.-C. (2009) 'Climate change and capture fisheries: potential impacts, adaptation and mitigation', in K. Cochrane, C. de Young, D. Soto and T. Bahri (eds) *Climate change implications for fisheries and aquaculture: overview of current scientific knowledge*, FAO Fisheries and Aquaculture Technical Paper No 530, Rome, FAO, pp107–150.

Department for Environment, Food and Rural Affairs (2006) *Economic Note on UK Grocery Retailing*, Food and Drink Economics Branch, DEFRA.

DeSilva, S.S. and Soto, D. (2009) 'Climate change and aquaculture: potential impacts, adaptation and mitigation', in K. Cochrane, C. de Young, D. Soto and T. Bahri (eds) *Climate change implications for fisheries and aquaculture: overview of current scientific knowledge*, FAO Fisheries and Aquaculture Technical Paper No 530, Rome, FAO, pp151–212.

DiNardo, G., Levy, D. and Golden, B. (1989) 'Using decision analysis to manage Maryland's river herring fishery: an application of AHP', *Journal of Environmental Management*, vol 29, pp193–213.

Ellis, G.M. and Fisher, A.C. (1987) 'Valuing the environment as input', *Journal of Environmental Management*, vol 25, pp149–156.

Engle, C.R. and Neira, I. (2005) *Tilapia Farm Business Management and Economics: a Training Manual*, Pine Bluff University of Arkansas.

EUROSTAT (2010) Eurostat database, http://ec.europa.eu/eurostat.

FAO (2008a) 'Report of the Expert Consultation on the Assessment of Socio-economic impacts of Aquaculture', Ankara, Turkey, 4–8 February 2008, FAO Fisheries Report No 861, Rome, FAO.

FAO (2008b) 'Report of the FAO Expert Workshop on Climate Change Implications for Fisheries and Aquaculture', Rome, Italy, 7–9 April 2008, FAO Fisheries Report No 870, Rome, FAO.

FAO (2009) *The State of World Fisheries and Aquaculture, 2008*, Rome, FAO Fisheries and Aquaculture Department.

FAO (2010a) *FishStat Database*, www.fao.org/fishery/statistics/programme/3,1,1/en.

FAO (2010b) *FAO Food Security Statistics*, www.fao.org/economic/ess/food-security-statistics/en/.

FAO Fisheries Department (2003) 'Fisheries Management 2: The ecosystem approach to fisheries', FAO Technical Guidelines for Responsible Fisheries No 4, Suppl 2, Rome, FAO.

Farber, S. and Costanza, R. (1987) 'The economic value of wetland ecosystems', *Journal of Environmental Management*, vol 24, pp41–51.

Fousekis, P. and Revell, B.J. (2005) 'Retail fish demand in Great Britain and its fisheries management implications', *Marine Resource Economics*, vol 19, pp495–510.

Fox, W.W. (1970) 'An Exponential Yield Model for Optimizing Exploited Fish Populations', *Transactions of the American Fisheries Society*, vol 99, pp80–88.

Freeman, A.M. (1991) 'Valuing environmental resources under alternative management regimes', *Ecological Economics*, vol 3, pp247–256.

García Negro, M.C., Villasante, S., Carballo Penela, A. and Rodríguez Rodríguez, G. (2009) 'Estimating the economic impact of the Prestige oil spill on the Death Coast (NW Spain) fisheries', *Marine Policy*, vol 33, pp8–23.

Garrod, B.G. and Whitmarsh, D.J. (1991) 'Computer spreadsheets and the appraisal of fisheries development projects: introductory exercises for education and training', *Project Appraisal*, vol 6, no 3, pp159–168.

Garza, M.D., Prada, A., Varela, M. et al (2009) 'Indirect assessment of economic damages from the Prestige oil spill: consequences for liability and risk prevention', *Disasters*, vol 33, no 1, pp95–99.

Garza-Gil, M.D., Prada-Blanco, A. and Vasquez-Rodriguez, X. (2006) 'Estimating the short-term economic damages from the *Prestige* oil spill in the Galician fisheries and tourism', *Ecological Economics*, vol 58, pp842–849.

Garza-Gil, M.D., Suris-Regueiro, J.C. and Varela-Lafuente, M.M. (2006) 'Assessment of economic damages from the *Prestige* oil spill', *Marine Policy*, vol 30, no 5, pp544–551.

Gittinger, J.P. (1982) *Economic Analysis of Agricultural Projects*, 2nd edn, Baltimore and London, Johns Hopkins University Press.

Glenn, H., Wattage, P., Mardle, S., Van Rensburg, T., Grehan, A. and Foley, N. (2010) 'Marine Protected Areas – substantiating their worth', *Marine Policy*, vol 34, pp421–430.

Gordon, H. (1954) 'The economic theory of a common property resource: the fishery', *Journal of Political Economy*, vol 62, pp124–142.

Grigalunas, T.A. and Congar, R. (eds) (1995) *Environmental Economics for Integrated Coastal Area Management: Valuation Methods and Policy Instruments*, UNEP Regional Seas Reports and Studies No 164.

Grigalunas, T., Anderson, R., Brown, G. et al (1986) 'Estimating the cost of oil spills: lessons from the *Amoco Cadiz* incident', *Marine Resource Economics*, vol 2, no 3, pp239–262.

Halide, H., Stigebrandt, A., Rehbein, M. and McKinnon, A.D. (2009) 'Developing a decision-support system for sustainable cage aquaculture', *Environmental Modelling and Software*, vol 24, pp694–702.

Hanley, N., Shogren, J.F. and White, B. (2001) *Introduction to Environmental Economics*, Oxford University Press.

Hannesson, R. (1993) *Bioeconomic Analysis of Fisheries*, Fishing News Books.

Herath, G. (2004) 'Incorporating community objectives in improved wetland management: the use of the analytic hierarchy process', *Journal of Environmental Management*, vol 70, pp263–273.

Hermann, R.O., Rauniyar, G.P., Hanson, G.D. and Wang, G. (1994) 'Identifying frequent seafood purchasers in the Northeastern U.S.', *Agricultural and Resource Economics Review*, vol 14, pp226–235.

Himes, A. (2007) 'Performance Indicator Importance in MPA Management Using a Multi-Criteria Approach', *Coastal Management*, vol 35, pp601–618.

Holland, D.S., Sanchirico, J.N., Johnston, R.J. and Joglekar, D. (2010) *Ecosystem Analysis for Ecosystem-based management*, Washington, DC and London, RFF Press.

Holland, D. and Wessells, C.R. (1998) 'Predicting consumer preferences for fresh salmon: the influence of safety inspection and production method attributes', *Agricultural and Resource Economics Review*, vol 27, pp1–14.

Holland, P. (2002) 'The Commercial Sector', in T. Hundloe (ed.) *Valuing Fisheries: an Economic Framework*, University of Queensland Press.

Holmer, M., Perez, M. and Duarte, C.M. (2003) 'Benthic primary producers – a neglected environmental problem in Mediterranean maricultures?', *Marine Pollution Bulletin*, vol 46, pp1372–1376.

Holmer, M., Black, K., Duarte, C.M. et al (eds) (2008) *Aquaculture in the Ecosystem*, New York, Springer-Verlag.

Huang, C.-H. (1990) 'Economic valuation of underground water and man-induced subsidence in aquaculture', *Applied Economics*, vol 22, pp31–43.

ICES (2010) Fish Statistics Database, International Council for the Exploration of the Seas, www.ices.dk.

ICTSD (2006) 'Fisheries, International Trade and Sustainable Development', Policy Discussion Paper, ICTSD Natural Resources, International Trade and Sustainable Development Series, Geneva, International Centre for Trade and Sustainable Development.

IMF (2009) *World Economic Outlook*, International Monetary Fund, www.imf.org/external/pubs/ft/weo/2009/01/pdf/text.pdf.

Innes, J.P. and Pascoe, S. (2010) 'A multi-criteria assessment of fishing gear impacts in demersal fisheries', *Journal of Environmental Management*, vol 91, pp932–939.

ITOPF (2010) *Statistics*, International Tanker Owners Pollution Federation, www.itopf.com/information-services/data-and-statistics/.

Jaffry, S.A., Pascoe, S. and Robinson, C. (1999) 'Long run price flexibilities for high valued UK fish species: a cointegration systems approach', *Applied Economics*, vol 31, pp473–481.

Jaffry, S., Pickering, H., Ghulam, Y., Whitmarsh, D. and Wattage, P. (2004) 'Consumer choices for quality and sustainability labelled seafood products in the UK', *Food Policy*, vol 29, pp215–228.

Jin, D., Thunberg, E. and Hoagland, P. (2008) 'Economic impact of the 2005 red tide event on commercial shellfish fisheries in New England', *Ocean and Coastal Management*, vol 51, pp420–429.

Judge, G. (1999) 'Simple Monte Carlo studies on a spreadsheet', *Computers in Higher Education Economics Review*, vol 13, no 2, pp12–14.

Kalof, L. and Satterfield, T. (eds) (2005) *The Earthscan Reader in Environmental Values*, London, Earthscan.

Kam, L. and Leung, P. (2008) 'Financial risk analysis in aquaculture', in M.G. Bondad-Reantaso, J.R. Arthur and R.G. Subasinghe (eds) *Understanding and applying risk analysis in aquaculture*. FAO Fisheries and Aquaculture Technical Paper No 519, Rome, FAO.

Kangas, J. (1995) 'Supporting the choice of the sports fishing site', *Journal of Environmental Management*, vol 43, pp219–231.

Katranidis, S., Nitsi, E. and Vakrou, A. (2003) 'Social acceptability of aquaculture development in coastal areas: the case of two Greek islands', *Coastal Management*, vol 31, pp37–53.

Knowler, D., Barbier, E.B. and Strand, I. (2001) 'An open-access model of fisheries and nutrient enrichment in the Black Sea', *Marine Resource Economics*, vol 16, pp195–217.

Knowler, D., Barbier, E.B. and Strand, I. (2002) 'An open-access model of fisheries and nutrient enrichment in the Black Sea: Errata', *Marine Resource Economics*, vol 17, pp347–349.

Kurien, J. (2005) 'Responsible Fish Trade and Food Security', FAO Fisheries Technical Paper No 456, Rome, FAO.

Lane, D.E. (2007) 'Planning in fisheries-related systems', in A. Weintraub, C. Romero, T. Bjorndal and R. Epstein (eds) *Handbook of Operations Research in Natural Resources*, New York, Springer Science and Business Media, pp237–271.

Ledoux, L. and Turner, R.K. (2002) 'Valuing ocean and coastal resources: a review of practical examples and issues for further action', *Ocean and Coastal Management*, vol 45, pp583–616.

Leeworthy, V.R. and Wiley, P.C. (1996) *Importance and satisfaction ratings by recreating visitors to the Florida Keys/Key West*, Silver Spring, MD, National Oceanic and Atmosphere Administration.

Leeworthy, V.R. and Wiley, P.C. (1997) *A socioeconomic analysis of the recreation activities of Monroe County residents in the Florida Keys/Key West*, Silver Spring, Maryland: National Oceanic and Atmosphere Administration.

Leung, P. (2006) 'Multiple-criteria decision-making (MCDM) applications in fishery management', *International Journal of Environmental Technology and Management*, vol 6, nos 1/2, pp96–110.

Leung, P., Muraoka, J., Nakamoto, S.T. and Pooley, S. (1998) 'Evaluating fisheries management options in Hawaii using analytic hierarchy process (AHP)', *Fisheries Research*, vol 36, pp171–183.

Lipton, D. and Strand, I. (1997) 'Economic effects of pollution in fish habitats', *Transactions of the American Fisheries Society*, vol 126, pp514–518.

Lorenzen, K. (2005) 'Population dynamics and potential fisheries stock enhancement: practical theory for assessment and policy analysis', *Phil. Trans. R. Soc. B.*, vol 360, pp171–189.

Loureiro, M.L., Loomis, J.B. and Vasquez, M.X. (2009) 'Economic valuation of environmental damages due to the *Prestige* oil spill in Spain', *Environmental and Resource Economics*, vol 44, pp537–553.

Loureiro, M.L., Ribas, A., Lopez, E. and Ojea, E. (2006) 'Estimated costs and admissible claims linked to the *Prestige* oil spill', *Ecological Economics*, vol 59, pp48–63.

Lynne, G.D., Conroy, P. and Prochaska, F.J. (1981) 'Economic value of marsh areas for production processes', *J. Env. Econ. Management*, vol 8, pp175–186.

Manning, P. (2005) 'The Namibian Hake Fishery', in S. Cunningham and T. Bostock (eds) *Successful Fisheries Management: Issues, Case Studies and Perspectives*, Delft, Eburon.

Mardle, S., Pascoe, S. and Herrero, I. (2004) 'Management objective importance in fisheries: an evaluation using the Analytic Hierarchy Process', *Environmental Management*, vol 33, no 1, pp1–11.

McCracken, J., Pretty, J. and Conway, G. (1988) *An introduction to rapid rural appraisal for agricultural development*, Sustainable Agriculture Program, London, International Institute for Environment and Development (IIED).

Milazzo, M. (1998) 'Subsidies in World Fisheries: A re-examination', World Bank Technical Paper No 406, Fisheries Series, Washington, DC, World Bank.

Moore, L.Y., Footit, A.J., Reynolds, L.M., Postle, M.G., Floyd, P.J., Fenn, T. and Virani, S. (1998) *Sea Empress Cost-Benefit Project. Environment Agency R&D Technical Report P119*, Bristol, Environment Agency.

MPP-EAS (1999) *Natural Resource Damage Assessment Manual*, GEF/UNDP/IMO Regional Programme for the Prevention and Management of Marine Pollution in the East Asian Sea, Quezon City, Philippines.

Muir, J. (2005) 'Managing to harvest? Perspectives on the potential of aquaculture', *Phil. Trans. R. Soc. B.*, vol 360, pp191–218.

Nauman, F.A., Gempesaw, C.M., Bacon, J.R. and Manalo, A. (1995) 'Consumer choice for fresh fish: factors affecting purchase decisions', *Marine Resource Economics*, vol 10, pp117–142.

Naylor, R., Goldburg, R., Mooney, H. et al (1998) 'Nature's subsidies to shrimp and salmon farming', *Science*, vol 282, pp883–884.

Nielsen, J.R. and Mathiesen, C. (2006) 'Stakeholder preferences for Danish fisheries management of sand eel and Norway pout', *Fisheries Research*, vol 77, pp92–101.

Olesen, I., Alfnes, F., Rora, M.B. and Kolstad, K. (2010) 'Eliciting consumers' willingness to pay for organic and welfare-labelled salmon in a non-hypothetical choice experiment', *Livestock Science*, vol 127, pp218–226.

Ostrom, E. (2008) 'Institutions and the environment', *Economic Affairs*, September.

Pascoe, S. (1997) 'Bycatch management and the economics of discarding', FAO Fisheries Technical Paper No 370, Rome, FAO.

Pascoe, S., Bustamante, R., Wilcox, C. and Gibbs, M. (2009) 'Spatial fisheries management: a framework for multi-objective qualitative assessment', *Ocean and Coastal Management*, vol 52, pp130–138.

Pascoe, S., Proctor, W., Wilcox, C. et al (2009) 'Stakeholder objective preferences in Australian Commonwealth managed fisheries', *Marine Policy*, vol 33, pp750–758.

Pauly, D., Christensen, V., Guenette, S. et al (2002) 'Towards sustainability in world fisheries', *Nature*, vol 418, pp689–695.

Pearce, D.W. and Moran, D. (1994) *The Economic Value of Biodiversity*, London, Earthscan.

Pickering, H., Whitmarsh, D. and Jensen, A. (1999) 'Artificial reefs as a tool to aid rehabilitation of coastal ecosystems: investigating the potential', *Marine Pollution Bulletin*, vol 37, nos 8–12, pp505–514.

Pipitone, C.F., Badalamenti, F., D'Anna, G. et al (2000) 'Trawling ban in the Gulf of Castellemmare: Effects on the Small-Scale Fishery Economics and on the Abundance of Fish', Study No 97/063, Final Report to the European Commission.

Pomeroy, R.S. (1992) 'Economic Studies of Small-Scale Fishers: a comparison of methodologies', *Asian Fisheries Science*, vol 5, pp63–72.

Pope, J. (1997) 'Integrating and presenting scientific fisheries management advice for complex fisheries subject to multiple objectives', in C.C. Monteiro. (ed.) *Multiple Objectives and Fisheries Management: Strategies for the Future*, Vilamoura International Meeting on Fisheries, Portugal, 3–4 November.

Ramos, J., Santos, M.N., Whitmarsh, D. and Monteiro, C.C. (2006) 'The usefulness of the analytic hierarchy process to understand reef diving choices: a case study', *Bulletin of Marine Science*, vol 78, no 1, pp213–219.

Read, P. and Fernandes, T. (2003) 'Management of environmental impacts of marine aquaculture in Europe', *Aquaculture*, vol 226, pp139–163.

Remoundou, K., Koundouri, P., Kontogianni, A. et al (2009) 'Valuation of natural marine ecosystems: an economic perspective', *Environmental Science and Policy*, vol 12, pp1040–1051.

Royal Commission on Environmental Pollution, (1998) *Setting Environmental Standards*, Twenty First Report, Cm 4053.

Saarni, K., Setala, J. and Honkanen, A. (2001) 'An application of AHP to strategic planning: improvement of quality of fish products', Paper presented at the XIIIth Conference of the European Association of Fisheries Economists (EAFE), Salerno, Italy, 18–20 April.

Saaty, T.L. (1977) 'A Scaling Method for Priorities in Hierarchical Structures', *Journal of Mathematical Psychology*, vol 15, no 3, pp234–281.

Saaty, T.L. and Vargas, L.G. (2000) *Models, Methods, Concepts and Applications of the Analytic Hierarchy Process*, Boston, Kluwer.

Sanchirico, J.N. (2000) 'Marine Protected Areas as fishery policy: discussion of potential costs and benefits', Discussion Paper 00-23, Resources for the Future, Washington, DC.

Sanchirico, J.N., Cochran, K.A. and Emerson, P.M. (2002) 'Marine Protected Areas: economic and social implications', Discussion Paper 02-26, Resources for the Future, Washington, DC.

Sathiendrakumar, R. and Tisdell, C.A. (1997) 'Optimal Economic Fishery Effort in the Maldivian Tuna Fishery: An Appropriate Model', *Marine Resource Economics*, vol 4, no 1, pp15–44.

Sathirathai, S. (1998) 'Economic valuation of mangroves and the roles of local communities in the conservation of resources: case study of Surat Thani, South of Thailand', Final Report Submitted to the Economy and Environment Program for Southeast Asia (EEP-SEA), Singapore.

Sathirathai, S. and Barbier, E.B. (2001) 'Valuing mangrove conservation in Southern Thailand', *Contemporary Economic Policy*, vol 19, pp109–122.

Schaefer, M. (1954) 'Some aspects of the dynamics population important to the management of the commercial marine fisheries', *Inter-American Tropical Tuna Commission Bulletin*, vol 1, pp27–56.

Scott, A. (2008) *The Evolution of Resource Property Rights*, Oxford, OUP.

Sea Fish Industry Authority (2010) *Retailing*, SFIA, www.seafish.org/land/chain.asp?p=fb206.

Seila, A.F. and Banks, J. (1990) 'Spreadsheet risk analysis using simulation', *Simulation*, vol 55, pp163–170.

Setala, J., Saarni, K. and Honkanen, A. (2000) 'The quality perceptions of rainbow trout defined by different fish market sectors', Paper presented at the Tenth Biennial Conference of the International Institute of Fisheries Economics and Trade (IIFET), Corvallis, Oregon, 10–15 July.

Shah, M.A. and Sharma, U. (2003) 'Optimal harvesting policies for a generalized Gordon–Schaefer model in randomly varying environment', *Applied Stochastic Models in Business and Industry*, vol 19, no 1, pp43–49.

Shang, Y.C. (1981) *Aquaculture Economics: Basic Concepts and Methods of Analysis*, Boulder, Colorado, Westview Press.

Sinan, H. and Whitmarsh, D. (2010) 'Wealth-based fisheries management and resource rent capture: an application to the Maldives marine fisheries', *Marine Policy*, vol 34, pp389–394.

Smith, D.J. (2000) 'Risk simulation and the appraisal of investment projects', *Computers in Higher Education Economics Review*, vol 14, pp9–13.

SOFIA (2008) 'The Status of World Fisheries and Aquaculture', FAO Corporate Document Repository, www.fao.org/docrep/011/i0250e/i0250e00. HTM.

Soma, K. (2003) 'How to involve stakeholders in fisheries management – a country case study in Trinidad and Tobago', *Marine Policy*, vol 27, pp47–58.

South Wales Sea Fisheries District Committee (2010) Landing Statistics, SWSFDC, www.swsfc.org.uk/home.htm.

Spurgeon, J. (1998) 'The socio-economic costs and benefits of coastal habitat rehabilitation and creation', *Marine Pollution Bulletin*, vol 37, pp373–382.

Sumaila, U.R., Khan, A., Watson, R. et al (2007) 'The World Trade Organization and global fisheries sustainability', *Fisheries Research*, vol 88, pp1–4.

Suris-Regueiro, J.C., Garza-Gil, M.D. and Varela-Lafuente, M. (2007) 'The *Prestige* oil spill and its economic impact on the Galician fishing sector', *Disasters*, vol 31, no 2, pp201–215.

Thebaud, O., Bailly, D., Hay, J. and Perez, J. (2004) 'The cost of oil pollution at sea: an analysis of the process of damage valuation and compensation following oil spills', in A. Prada and M.X. Vasquez (eds) *Economic, Social and Environmental Effects of the Prestige Oil Spill*, Santiago de Compostella, pp187–219.

Thorpe, A., Whitmarsh, D. and Failler, P. (2007) 'The Situation in World Fisheries', in *Encyclopedia of Life Support Systems (EOLSS)*, developed under the Auspices of the UNESCO, Oxford, Eolss Publishers.

Tingley, D., Stepleton, M., Esseen, M. and Seymour, T. (1998) *The Economics of Whelk Fishing*, Lymington, MacAlister Elliott & Partners

Tol, R.S.J. (2009) 'The economic effects of climate change', *Journal of Economic Perspectives*, vol 23, no 2, pp29–51.

Townsley, P. (1996) 'Rapid rural appraisal, participatory rural appraisal and aquaculture', FAO Fisheries Technical Paper No 358, Rome, FAO.

Trondsen, T., Scholderer, J., Lund, E. and Eggen, A.E. (2003) 'Perceived barriers to consumption of fish among Norwegian women', *Appetite*, vol 41, pp301–314.

Turner, R.K. and Adger, W.N. (1996) 'Coastal Resources Assessment Guidelines', LOICZ/R&S/96-4.

Tveteras, S. and Tveteras, R. (2010) 'The global competition for wild fish resources between livestock and aquaculture', *Journal of Agricultural Economics*, vol 61, no 2, pp381–397.

US Department of Commerce, National Oceanographic and Atmospheric Administration, (1983) 'Assessing the Social Costs of Oil Spills: the Amoco Cadiz Case Study', Washington, DC.

Utne, I.B. (2008) 'Are the smallest fishing vessels the most sustainable? Trade-off analysis of sustainability attributes', *Marine Policy*, vol 32, pp465–474.

Valatin, G. (2000) 'Demand-side approaches to Solving the "Tragedy of High Prices" in Fisheries', IIFET Conference Paper.

Wattage P. and Mardle S. (2005) 'Stakeholder preferences towards conservation versus development for a wetland in Sri Lanka', *Journal of Environmental Management*, vol 77, pp122–132.

Wattage, P. and Mardle, S. (2006) 'Valuing wetland resources using the analytic hierarchy process', in G. Herath and T. Prato (eds) *Using Multi-Criteria Decision Analysis in Natural Resource Management*, Aldershot, Ashgate.

Welcomme, R.L. (1996) 'Definitions of aquaculture and intensification of production from fisheries', *FAO Aquaculture Newsletter*, vol 12, pp3–5.

Welcomme, R.L. and Bartley, D.M. (1998) 'Current approaches to the enhancement of fisheries', *Fisheries Management and Ecology*, vol 5, pp351–382.

Whitmarsh, D. (1997) 'Socio-economic implications of alternative fisheries management strategies', in C.C. Monteiro (ed.) *Multiple Objectives and Fisheries Management: Strategies for the Future*, Vilamoura International Meeting on Fisheries, Portugal, 3–4 November.

Whitmarsh, D. and Palmieri, M.G. (2008) 'Aquaculture in the Coastal Zone: pressures, interactions and externalities', in M. Holmer et al (eds) *Aquaculture in the Ecosystem*, Springer.

Whitmarsh, D. and Palmieri, M.G. (2009) 'Social acceptability of marine aquaculture: the use of survey-based methods for eliciting public and stakeholder preferences', *Marine Policy*, vol 33, pp452–457.

Whitmarsh, D. and Seijo, J.C. (2007) 'Economics of Aquaculture', in P. Safran (ed.) *Fisheries and Aquaculture, Encyclopedia of Life Support Systems (EOLSS)*, Developed under the Auspices of the UNESCO, Oxford, Eolss Publishers.

Whitmarsh, D. and Wattage, P. (2006) 'Public attitudes towards the environmental impact of salmon aquaculture in Scotland', *European Environment*, vol 16, no 2, pp108–121.

Whitmarsh, D., James, C., Pickering, H. and Neiland, A. (2000) 'The profitability of marine commercial fisheries: a review of economic information needs with particular reference to the UK', *Marine Policy*, vol 24, no 3, pp257–263.

Whitmarsh, D., Reid, C., Dunn, M. and Gulvin, C. (1995) 'Natural resource exploitation and the role of new technology: a case history of the UK herring industry', *Environmental Conservation*, vol 22, no 2, pp103–110.

Wilen, J.E. (2006) 'Why fisheries management fails: treating the symptoms rather than the cause', *Bulletin of Marine Science*, vol 78, no 3, pp529–546.

World Bank (2006) 'Aquaculture: Changing the Face of the Waters. Meeting the Promise and Challenge of Sustainable Aquaculture', Report 36622-GLB.

World Bank and FAO (2009) *The Sunken Billions: the Economic Justification for Fisheries Reform*, Washington, International Bank for Reconstruction and Development.

Worm, B., Barbier, E.B., Beaumont, N. et al (2006) 'Impacts of Biodiversity Loss on Ocean Ecosystem Services', *Science*, vol 314, no 5800, pp787–790.

Worm, B., Hilborn, R., Baum, J.K. et al (2009) 'Rebuilding Global Fisheries', *Science*, vol 325, no 5940, pp578–585.

Young, J.A., Brugere, C. and Muir, J.F. (1999) 'Green grow the fishes-oh? Environmental attributes in marketing aquaculture products', *Aquaculture Economics and Management*, vol 3, no 1, pp7–17.

Further Reading

Anderson, L. (1987) 'Expansion of the fisheries management paradigm to include institutional structure and function', *Transactions of the American Fisheries Society*, vol 116, no 3, pp396–404.

Arnason, R. (1998) 'Ocean fisheries management: implications for the volume and quality of fish supply', *Fisheries Research*, vol 34, pp215–225.

Bailey, C. (1988) 'The political economy of fisheries development in the third world', *Agriculture and Human Values*, Winter–Spring, pp35–48.

Barbier, E.B. and Cox, M. (2004) 'An economic analysis of shrimp farm expansion and mangrove conversion in Thailand', *Land Economics*, vol 80, pp389–407.

Barbier, E.B. and Strand, I. (1998) 'Valuing mangrove-fishery linkages. A case study of Campeche, Mexico', *Environmental and Resource Economics*, vol 12, pp151–166.

Bell, F. (1972) 'Technological externalities and common property resources: an empirical study of the US northern lobster fishery', *Journal of Political Economy*, vol 80, pp148–158.

Béné, C. (2003) 'When Fisheries Rhymes with Poverty: A First Step beyond the Old Paradigm of Poverty in Small-Scale Fisheries', *World Development*, vol 31, no 6, pp949–975.

Béné, C. and Heck, S. (2005) *Fish and Food Security in Africa*, Penang, The WorldFish Center.

Bjorndal, T. and Conrad, J. (1987) 'The dynamics of an open access fishery', *Canadian Journal of Economics*, vol 20, no 1, pp74–85.

Christy, F. (1996) 'The death rattle of open access and the advent of property rights regimes in fisheries', *Marine Resource Economics*, vol 11, pp287–304.

Clark, C.W., Munro, G. and Sumaila, U.R. (2005) 'Subsidies, buybacks, and sustainable fisheries', *Journal of Environmental Economics and Management*, pp47–58.

Clark, C.W., Munro, G. and Sumaila, U.R. (2010) 'Limits to the privatization of fishery resources', *Land Economics*, vol 86, no 2, pp209–218.

Collins, A., Stapleton, M. and Whitmarsh, D. (1998) 'Fishery-pollution interactions: a modelling approach to exploring the nature and incidence of economic damages', *Marine Pollution Bulletin*, vol 36, no 3, pp211–221.

Copes, P. (1986) 'A critical review of the individual quota as a device in fisheries management', *Land Economics*, vol 62, no 3, pp278–291.

Cunningham, S. (1994) 'Fishermen's incomes and fisheries management', *Marine Resource Economics*, vol 9, no 3, pp241–262.

Dalzell, P. et al (1987) 'Estimation of Maximum Sustainable Yield and Maximum Economic Rent from the Philippine Small Pelagic Fisheries', ICLARM and BFAR Technical Paper Series X(3).

Failler, P. and Kane, A. (2003) 'Sustainable Livelihood Approach and Improvement of the Living Conditions of Fishing Communities: Relevance, Applicability and Applications', in A. Neiland and C. Béné (eds) *Fishery and Poverty*, London, Kluwer, pp121–149.

Grainger, R. and Garcia, S. (1996) 'Chronicles of marine fishery landings (1950–1994): Trend analysis and fisheries potential', FAO Fisheries Technical Paper 359, Rome, FAO.

Grigalunas, T., Opaluch, J., Diamantides, J. and Mazzotta, M. (1998) 'Liability for oil spill damages: issues, methods and examples', *Coastal Management*, vol 26, pp61–77.

Hannesson, R. (1988) 'Optimum Fishing Effort and Economic Rent: a case study of Cyprus', FAO Fisheries Technical Paper 299.

Hannesson, R. (1998) 'Marine Reserves – what would they accomplish?', *Marine Resource Economics*, vol 13, pp159–170.

Hilborn, R. (2007) 'Defining success in fisheries and conflicts in objectives', *Marine Policy*, vol 31, no 2, pp153–158.

Israel, D.C. and Banzon, C.P. (1997) 'Overfishing in the Philippine Commercial Marine Fisheries Sector', Philippine Institute for Development Studies, Discussion Paper Series No 97-01.

Jin, D., Thunberg, E. and Hoagland, P. (2008) 'Economic impact of the red tide event on commercial shellfish fisheries in New England', *Ocean and Coastal Management*, vol 51, pp420–429.

Kent, G. (1997) 'Fisheries, food security and the poor', *Food Policy*, vol 22, no 5, pp393–404.

Mardle, S., Pascoe, S., Boncoeur, J. et al (2002) 'Objectives of fisheries management: case studies from the UK, France, Spain and Denmark', *Marine Policy*, vol 26, no 6, pp415–428.

Neiland, A.E. and Béné, C. (2004) (eds) *Poverty and Small-Scale Fisheries in West Africa*, Rome, FAO; Dordrecht, Kluwer.

OECD (1997) *Towards Sustainable Fisheries: Economic Aspects of the Management of Living Marine Resources*, Paris, OECD.

OECD (2006) *Using Market Mechanisms to Manage Fisheries: Smoothing the Path*, Paris OECD.

Panayotou, T. and Jetanavanich, S. (1987) 'The Economics and Management of Thai Marine Fisheries', *ICLARM Studies and Reviews*, no 14.

Pauly, D., Christensen, V., Guenette, S. et al (2002) 'Towards sustainability in world fisheries', *Nature*, vol 418, pp689–695.

Platteau, J.-P. (1989) 'The Dynamics of Fisheries Development in Developing Countries: A General Overview', *Development and Change*, vol 20, pp565–597.

Sathirathai, S. and Barbier, E.B. (2001) 'Valuing mangrove conservation in Southern Thailand', *Contemporary Economic Policy*, vol 19 pp109–122.

Sharp, R. and Sumaila, U.R. (2009) 'Quantification of U.S. Marine Fisheries Subsidies', *North American Journal of Fisheries Management*, vol 29, pp18–32.

Shotton, R. (ed.) (2000) 'Use of Property Rights in Fisheries Management', FAO Technical Paper 404/1, Rome, FAO.

Shotton, R. (ed.) (2001) 'Case Studies on the Allocation of Transferable Quota Rights in Fisheries', FAO Technical Paper 411, Rome, FAO.

Spurgeon, J. (1998) 'The socio-economic costs and benefits of coastal rehabilitation and creation', *Marine Pollution Bulletin*, vol 37, nos 8–12, pp373–382.

Thorpe, A. (2005) 'Mainstreaming Fisheries into National Development and Poverty Reduction Strategies: Current Situation and Opportunities', Fisheries Circular No 997, Rome, FAO.

Thorpe, A., Andrew, N.L. and Allison, E.H. (2007) 'Fisheries and Poverty Reduction', *CAB Reviews: Perspectives in Agriculture, Veterinary Science, Nutrition and Natural Resources*, vol 2, no 85, pp1–12.

Thorpe, A., Reid, C., van Anrooy and R. Brugére, C. (2005) 'African Poverty Reduction Strategy Programmes and the Fisheries Sector: Current Situation and Opportunities', *African Development Review*, vol 16, pp328–362.

Thorpe, A., Reid, C., van Anrooy, R. and Brugere, C. (2005) 'When Fisheries influence National Policy-Making: An Analysis of the National Development Strategies of Major Fish-Producing Nations in the Developing World', *Marine Policy*, vol 29, pp211–222.

Thorpe, A., Reid, C., van Anrooy, R. et al (2006) 'Poverty Reduction Strategy Papers and the Fisheries Sector An Opportunity Forgone', *Journal of International Development*, vol 17, pp1–29.

Tran Thanh Be, Le Canh Dung and Brenan, D. (1999) 'Environmental costs of shrimp farming in the rice-growing regions of the Mekong Delta', *Aquaculture Economics and Management*, vol 3, pp31–42.

von Moltke, A. (ed.) (2010) *Fisheries Subsidies, Sustainable Development and the WTO*, London, Earthscan.

Whitmarsh, D. (1990) 'Technological change and marine fisheries development', *Marine Policy*, vol 14, no 1, pp15–22.

Whitmarsh, D. (1998) 'The fisheries treadmill', *Land Economics*, vol 74, no 3, pp422–427.

Whitmarsh, D., James, C., Pickering, H. and Neiland, A. (2000) 'The profitability of marine commercial fisheries: a review of economic information needs with particular reference to the UK', *Marine Policy*, vol 24, no 3, pp257–263.

Whitmarsh, D., James, C., Pickering, H. et al (2002) 'Economic effects of fisheries exclusion zones: a Sicilian case study', *Marine Resource Economics*, vol 17, no 3, pp239–250.

Whitmarsh, D., Pipitone, C., Badalamenti, F. and D'Anna, G. (2003) 'The economic sustainability of artisanal fisheries: the case of the trawl ban in the Gulf of Castellammare, NW Sicily', *Marine Policy*, vol 27, no 6, pp489–497.

Whitmarsh, D., Ramos, J., Santos, M.N. and Monteiro, C.C. (2008) 'Marine habitat modification off the Algarve (southern Portugal): An economic analysis of the fisheries and the prospects for management', *Ocean and Coastal Management*, vol 51, pp463–468.

Worldfish Center (2005) *Fisheries and the Millennium Development Goals: Solutions for Africa*, Penang, Worldfish Center.

Index

Ollscoil na hÉireann, Gaillimh

3 1111 40280 3306